March 7, 2007

THE THIRD STAGE OF LIFE—
AGING IN CONTEMPORARY SOCIETY

The Third Stage of Life

Aging in Contemporary Society

Daisaku Ikeda

With
Osamu Matsuoka and
Katsusuke Sasaki of the
Seikyo Shimbun
and
KANEKO IKEDA

World Tribune
Press

Published by World Tribune Press
A division of the SGI-USA
606 Wilshire Blvd.
Santa Monica, CA 90401

Cover and interior design by Gopa & Ted2, Inc.

Interior photos from Japan courtesy of Seikyo Press. © Seikyo Press

Image of Leo Tolstoy on p. 12 by Ullstein Bild/Getty Images.

10 9 8 7 6 5 4 3 2 1

ISBN: 978-1-935523-97-0
Library of Congress Control Number: 2016933932

Contents

Preface to the Japanese Edition

The young are beautiful–but the old are
more beautiful than the young.
—Walt Whitman, "Debris"[1]

Nothing is more sublime and reinvigorating than the dignified look of those who have persevered through all the ups and downs of life's unfolding seasons.

With the ongoing graying of our society, I ventured to deal with some of the most pressing issues confronting us in "The Third Stage of Life: Aging in Contemporary Society," which was serialized in the *Seikyo Shimbun*.

I believe that there are two aspects that must be addressed to ensure that older people may live in unfettered dignity as they set out to conclude the final chapters of their lives. First is to address how the elderly themselves approach life, their choices and convictions, as they continue to age. Second is how society will support senior citizens through its various policies and initiatives.

The ancient Buddhist scripture, Sutta Nipata, states, "Though being well-to-do, not to support father and mother who are old and past their youth—this is a cause of one's downfall."

It seems to me that an aging society's true flourishing is closely tied to the establishment of an atmosphere of respect for the elderly. I have made a conscious effort to discuss this point in this work.

My mentor, Josei Toda, would often remark: "How you end your life is what counts. No matter what may have happened in the past, the true victor is happy and fulfilled to the very end. I hope my twilight years will be like a glorious sunset."

Mr. Toda's life was by no means a long one. His two-year-incarceration during World War II had taken a heavy toll on his health. Nevertheless, he was true to his word, leading a life that culminated in ultimate success, one made immortal by laying the firm foundations for kosen-rufu to advance worldwide.

The first president of the Soka Gakkai, Tsunesaburo Makiguchi, founded the organization, initiating our kosen-rufu movement, just before he turned sixty. While he would die in prison, his passing was most composed and dignified. He bequeathed to later generations the lofty spirit of giving one's life for a noble cause, ensuring that our movement shall advance and expand in perpetuity.

These two founding presidents have both shown us, without words, how to create the maximum value out of our lives until the very end.

Every day, I offer prayers for the safety and longevity of my treasured fellow members from the pioneering days of the Soka Gakkai, the men and women who have selflessly battled with me for the sake of kosen-rufu without regard for personal fame or profit. How can I ever forget them? They have always been close to my heart and it was primarily with them in mind that I began to engage in the discussions featured in this book.

Following the request from the Editorial Department, my wife, Kaneko, also participated in several of the discussions. It was the first time she agreed to do so. Our lives together have spanned half a century, a time of ceaseless struggle spent expressly on advancing kosen-rufu. We would therefore be grateful and pleased if our experiences would prove to be of some inspiration to our readers.

On the thirty-eighth anniversary of my first
visit overseas for worldwide kosen-rufu
Daisaku Ikeda
October 2, 1998

Editor's Note

In the summer of 1997, as he was nearing his seventieth birthday, SGI President Daisaku Ikeda began a series of conversations on aging with two senior *Seikyo Shimbun* staff: General Editorial Bureau Senior Director Osamu Matsuoka and Vice Director Katsusuke Sasaki. These conversations were serialized in the *Seikyo Shimbun*, the Soka Gakkai's daily newspaper in Japan, until March 1998. Kaneko Ikeda, the SGI president's wife, joined the later conversations.

These translations originally appeared in English in the *World Tribune* from November 1997 to November 1998.

The citations most commonly used in this book have been abbreviated as follows:

LSOC, page number(s) refers to *The Lotus Sutra and Its Opening and Closing Sutras*, translated by Burton Watson (Tokyo: Soka Gakkai, 2009).

OTT, page number(s) refers to *The Record of the Orally Transmitted Teachings*, translated by Burton Watson (Tokyo: Soka Gakkai, 2004).

WND, page number(s) refers to *The Writings of Nichiren Daishonin*, vol. 1 (WND-1) (Tokyo: Soka Gakkai, 1999) and vol. 2 (WND-2) (Tokyo, Soka Gakkai, 2006).

CHAPTER I

There Is No Retirement Age From Life

PRESIDENT IKEDA: Now that we have entered a time when average life expectancy has stretched into the eighties, it is important for us to consider how we can spend our senior years, the third stage of our lives, in the most fruitful and rewarding fashion. My beloved mentor, Josei Toda, the second Soka Gakkai president, used to say that the last years of our life are the most important. If those last few years are happy ones, we have had a happy life. The victories and achievements up to that time are all illusory; the person who wins in the end is a victor in the truest sense of the word.

How should we face and deal with the issues of aging, sickness, and death? I'm sure we will touch on many subjects in the course of our discussion. Let's examine them one by one.

MATSUOKA AND SASAKI: We look forward to it.

PRESIDENT IKEDA: Though we speak of "the third stage of life," there is no set age that marks our entry into this period. It basically means that we have reached an advanced age—the start of a stage or chapter where we put the finishing touches on our development and bring our lives to completion.

Japan has recently become the world's leader in terms of average life expectancy. How has the average life span changed in Japan over the years?

MATSUOKA: In the late nineteenth and early twentieth centuries, the average life span for both men and women reached forty. It pushed upward to fifty soon after World War II. Today, it has stretched to eighty.[2]

SASAKI: In Japan today, one in seven people is over sixty-five, but by 2020, it is estimated that number will have climbed to one in four.[3] Soon Japan will overtake Sweden as the nation with the largest elderly population in the world.

A Bright and Youthful Spirit No Matter What Your Age

PRESIDENT IKEDA: The elderly members who comprise the Soka Gakkai's Many Treasures Group have devoted their lives to kosen-rufu, working for the happiness of their fellow human beings and for the sake of Buddhism and peace. As a result, they enjoy the immeasurable good fortune of long life and the protection of all Buddhas throughout the universe; they are always youthful and energetic.

Though our bodies may age, by participating in SGI

activities our hearts and minds remain as bright and shining as the sun. We are youthful as long as we live. Those who work for others' happiness and for Buddhism remain vigorous and full of energy.

I am always praying for the noble men and women who have worked so hard over many long years to build the Soka Gakkai and the SGI. I pray for their health, their long life, and that they may spend their last years filled with a deep sense of satisfaction and accomplishment. It is to these worthy members, those who have walked together with me since the pioneering days of our movement, always devoted to our cause and never seeking personal gain, that I would like to dedicate this discussion series.

SASAKI: As a *Seikyo Shimbun* journalist, I have reported on many, many occasions when you spoke about the Buddhist teachings to people all around the world. Each time, I am deeply impressed by your great spirit to keep moving forward—facing each moment as a fresh new challenge.

PRESIDENT IKEDA: It is important to always look to the future, to have plans and aspirations, and it is a particularly crucial factor in making the last years of one's life rewarding and fulfilling ones.

MATSUOKA: In May 1997, you were named an honorary professor of Shanghai University. During his speech at the presentation ceremony, University Senior Vice Chancellor

Fang Minglun read a list of some of the distinguished figures you have held dialogues with over the years.

The Beauty of a Life of Mission

PRESIDENT IKEDA: Yes, I think he mentioned Zhou Enlai, Arnold Toynbee, Mikhail Sholokhov, Henry Kissinger, Aurelio Peccei, Norman Cousins, Nelson Mandela, among others. I found one thing that was true of all these individuals: the older they got, the more energetically they devoted themselves to their chosen work. Age made them only more impressive. All of them are or were wonderful human beings who dedicated their lives to their missions. The lives of those who move forward with such a sense of mission have a true majesty and beauty.

SASAKI: Between the two of us, Mr. Matsuoka and I have been fortunate to have reported on your dialogues with at least half of these people. In this discussion on the third stage of life, I hope you will share with us the ways in which those individuals may serve as models.

PRESIDENT IKEDA: Certainly. Please feel free to ask me anything. In the upcoming discussions, let us range far and plumb deep.

The Spirit of Leonardo da Vinci

MATSUOKA: You once visited the chateau where Leonardo da Vinci spent his last years.

PRESIDENT IKEDA: Yes, it was more than two decades ago. After my dialogue with Dr. Toynbee in London, I flew to Paris, and in the short time left to me before I was scheduled to return to Japan, I visited the Loire Valley, a center of the French Renaissance.

The valley is about two hours from Paris by train. Ancient castles dotting the hilltops here and there slumbered peacefully in the spring sunlight, and lambs and calves gamboled in the green fields. The pure waters of a rushing river washed rocky banks, and narrow trails winding through the forest were lined with irises and bright yellow mustard flowers.

SASAKI: The palace of the French king Francis I, who invited Leonardo to France, was located in Amboise. The great Italian artist and inventor took up residence nearby, in Cloux; it was there he spent his last years, and where he died.

MATSUOKA: A quotation of Leonardo is engraved on a copper plaque in the bedroom of his house. I remember you looked at the plaque for some time, President Ikeda, and then said: "Those are excellent words. Please write them down for me. . . ."

PRESIDENT IKEDA: I was deeply impressed by them because they seemed to represent the very essence of Leonardo's life, the soul of a genius who was the epitome of the Renaissance spirit. "As a day well spent brings happy sleep, so a life well used brings happy death."[4]

Leonardo is comparing the sound sleep after a full day with a tranquil death after a full life. Buddhism teaches that death is but an expedient means and that life itself continues.[5] Our day begins with an invigorated awakening, and at night we lay our tired body down for its much deserved rest. Refreshed by sleep, we wake again the next morning with renewed energy. Viewed in terms of the eternity of life, death is the first step on the journey to a new existence.

SASAKI: The writer Yasushi Inoue,[6] with whom you carried on a correspondence that was later published under the title *Letters of Four Seasons*, expressed a strong interest in those words of Leonardo. In a letter to you, he wrote:

> Among the three impressive sentences you found engraved on a copper tablet in the chateau, the last moves me most deeply: "A full life gives a tranquil death." I am certain this statement is especially applicable to artists who have lived full lives.[7]

PRESIDENT IKEDA: Mr. Inoue went on to say that he wanted to visit the chateau where Leonardo lived.

Leonardo, who continued to challenge himself throughout his life, also wrote: "Iron rusts when it is not used. Stagnant water loses its purity and freezes over with the cold; so, too, does inactivity sap the vigor of the mind."[8] I was also impressed that shortly before his death, he wrote the inspiring words, "I shall continue."[9]

SASAKI: Speaking of continuing, Dr. Toynbee's motto was *"Laboremus!"* (Let's get to work!), wasn't it?

PRESIDENT IKEDA: Yes. At the start of our dialogue he said to me: "Let's get to work! Let us engage in this dialogue for the sake of humanity in the twenty-first century!" When I asked him—and he was eighty-four at the time—what was the most fulfilling and happy time for him, he answered with a smile, "When I am writing and reading."

He rose each day at a quarter to seven in the morning. He and his wife prepared breakfast together. Then he made his bed and was sitting at his desk in his study by nine, starting to write. He still burned with a passion for knowledge, though he was well over eighty.

MATSUOKA: I had the opportunity to report on your dialogue with Dr. Toynbee at his home in Oakwood Court, London. I remember it well. Dr. Toynbee lived in a redbrick apartment building. You took an old-fashioned elevator up to the fifth floor. Dr. Toynbee was very eager for you to arrive, so he had come out to wait for you in front of the elevator. I remember how happy he was when the elevator doors opened. He greeted you joyfully with a broad smile, firmly grasped your hand, and ushered you into his living room.

SASAKI: Though you were as far apart in age as a parent and child, he seemed to have a great respect for you as an equal.

MATSUOKA: Each day the dialogue sessions lasted for five hours, from ten in the morning. The tall, white-haired

Mr. Ikeda's dialogue with the eminent British historian Arnold J. Toynbee in May 1973 in London later became a book titled Choose Life.

Dr. Toynbee participated with an intent expression on his face. He frequently interjected with expressions of joy and approval. When the subject turned to the theory of life and Buddhist philosophy, he solicited your opinion earnestly.

PRESIDENT IKEDA: Dr. Toynbee, who has been hailed as the greatest historian of the twentieth century, continued to study all his life. He told me, "In my eighty-four years, I have never engaged in a dialogue of this caliber." It seemed with each passing year his passion to learn and study grew stronger.

Unflagging Desire to Study and Grow

MATSUOKA: After those first series of dialogues in 1972 were completed, Dr. Toynbee turned to you and said with considerable emotion to the effect: "Speaking with you has been stimulating and moving. Talking so directly and openly with a person who is capable of discussing the truly important issues is of enormous value to me, and I have no greater joy as a scholar. What you have said is of great significance to human life, and not merely on the conceptual level, for you are also passionately committed to solving the actual problems we confront. This dialogue with you has allowed me to organize my own studies."

SASAKI: When you met Dr. Toynbee again for the second series of dialogues a year later in 1973, one of the first things the two of you spoke about was the pressing need to solve the issue of caring for the aged in modern industrial society.

PRESIDENT IKEDA: Yes, we did. In response to a question I posed about the situation in the United Kingdom, Dr. Toynbee remarked that senior citizens, including himself, drew a national pension, and that many people lived in what were called "old people's homes," commenting that his wife's sister lived in one that was run by the government. Dr. Toynbee strongly advocated the importance of extended families, with grandparents, parents, and children living under one roof. He also said that urban housing needed to be reconsidered to make that possible even in the cities.

He was a pioneering thinker. He had considered many issues that concern us today, such as the issue of the precise definition of death, the use of artificial life-support systems to prolong life, and the question of the quality of life.

MATSUOKA: Yes, we look forward to that very much.

PRESIDENT IKEDA: People like Dr. Toynbee and Leonardo da Vinci teach us that there is no retirement from challenging the issues before us, or from the quest to learn and lead a fulfilling life.

CHAPTER 2

Your True Character Is Ultimately Revealed in Your Face

PRESIDENT IKEDA: In your later years, your face reveals your true character. The years have made their mark there, and you cannot hide them. The eyes, in particular, eloquently reveal what kind of person you are. Nichiren writes, "The spirit within one's body of five or six feet may appear in just one's face, which is only a foot long, and the spirit within one's face may appear in just one's eyes, which are only an inch across" (WND-1, 922).

MATSUOKA: You have said that the face you most admire is that of the Russian author Tolstoy in his later years.

PRESIDENT IKEDA: Yes. Tolstoy's face in his later years was marvelous. The lofty essence of a great life was distilled in it. His clear eyes shone with a light from deep within, his gaze fixed on eternity and penetrating the truth of all phenomena. A long, gray beard graced his noble and mature countenance, which was filled with an expression of love for humanity. A face such as Tolstoy's only comes from a life

Leo Tolstoy, c. 1900.

that has withstood the buffeting of the fiercest elements, a life of struggle for truth and justice.

SASAKI: I remember when you visited Tolstoy's home, which has been preserved as the Tolstoy State Museum, in Moscow in 1981. There was a statue of Tolstoy as well as a portrait. You gazed intently at both of them. And I remember you asking the museum's director many pointed questions about Tolstoy's life as she showed us around the displays.

PRESIDENT IKEDA: The home of that great writer was extremely simple and plain compared to the gorgeous luxury of the Kremlin, symbol of the czars' power and authority in Tolstoy's day.

To the very end, surrounded by the Russian people whom he loved so dearly, Tolstoy dedicated his life to fighting against the authoritarianism of church and state.

MATSUOKA: Tolstoy was eighty-two when he passed away.

Writing Each Day Without Fail

PRESIDENT IKEDA: According to the museum director, even in his last years Tolstoy kept to a strict and rigorous schedule, writing every day from ten in the morning to three in the afternoon, even on holidays. On the very last journey he made just before his death, he continued to seek the meaning of life and bring an end to the spiritual turmoil that wracked him. He collapsed in an isolated country village in the midst of his travels. "On his deathbed he wept, not for himself, but for the unhappy," writes Romaine Rolland. "And he said, in the midst of his sobs: 'There are millions of human beings on earth who are suffering: why do you think only of me?'"[10]

The statue of Tolstoy that graces the main entrance of the Soka University Auditorium has been placed there out of the cherished hope that students of the university will emulate this great individual and continue to develop themselves and fight for the sake of the people to the very last day of their lives.

SASAKI: The Nobel Prize-winning author Mikhail A. Sholokhov (1905–84), whom you met, was apparently from a Cossack region in Russia. He had an unusual inner strength and vitality. We were told that he was ill, but when you went to meet him [in 1974], he was actually surprisingly well. I believe he was sixty-nine at the time.

PRESIDENT IKEDA: Yes, that's right. He had very good color, and though he was white-haired and rather small-framed, there was a definite aura of the depth of spirit and mettle of a literary giant. He urged me again and again to share a drink of cognac with him. I can't drink, and I kept trying to refuse politely. Finally, I pretended to take a drink and then passed the glass to you, who were sitting behind me.

SASAKI: Yes. I drank it for you. It was delicious. Thank you very much.

PRESIDENT IKEDA: At any rate, I distinctly remember his spirited nature. He remarked to the effect: "You can't accomplish anything worthwhile if you don't have a definite goal. We are all 'blacksmiths' who have to hammer and shape our own happiness. People of conviction, people who are spiritually strong, can exert a definite influence on the direction their lives take, even when fate takes an unexpected twist." In short, he believed that we each build our own happiness. He was a person of great energy and insight.

MATSUOKA: At that time, you were forty-six, but now you are the same age as Mr. Sholokhov when you first met. In the intervening years, you have faced challenge after challenge, growing in strength and dignity and offering a model for how we can all live the third stage of our lives to the fullest.

PRESIDENT IKEDA: All of those who have devoted themselves earnestly to propagating the correct teachings of Nichiren Daishonin are models. It is wonderful and noble to take the lead in working to help others, to exert oneself tirelessly for the sake of others' happiness. As it states in *The Record of the Orally Transmitted Teachings*, "The heavenly gods and benevolent deities will appear in the form of men and women" (OTT, 86). Those who work for kosen-rufu will enjoy the protection and support of all kinds of people in their environment.

SASAKI: At the beginning of 1975, you first met Dr. Henry Kissinger, former U.S. Secretary of State, at the State Department in Washington, D.C. Snow had been falling lightly since morning, and the trees were beautifully blanketed in white.

PRESIDENT IKEDA: I met with Dr. Kissinger on several occasions after that as well. We talked about many things, covering a broad range of topics from international crises to our philosophies of life. Eventually, our talks were published as a dialogue.[11] When we broached the subject of how to spend the years of our old age and the meaning of death, a comment by Dr. Kissinger made a deep impression on me. "I have always been impressed," he remarked, "by something the German statesman Bismark said. Bismark had been married for fifty years when his wife died. At her bedside, he said, 'It's only just started and now it's already over.' I think that is the poignancy of life with which everyone has to come to grips."

MATSUOKA: Bismark was married for fifty years, and you and Mrs. Ikeda will celebrate your fiftieth wedding anniversary on May 3, 2002, a golden anniversary.

PRESIDENT IKEDA: Mr. Toda selected the day May 3 for our wedding. There actually should have been a big general meeting to celebrate the first anniversary of his presidency on that day, but he decided that it should be our wedding day. There was no general meeting that year as a result. I have never for a moment forgotten the deep love and warm support that Mr. Toda bestowed on us.

MATSUOKA: In the past, you were interviewed by a Japanese women's magazine for its New Year's edition. There was one exchange I remember very well that went as follows:

INTERVIEWER: I have heard that you've been married for thirty-seven years. Having met your wife, I can see what a warm and kind person she is. If, looking back on your years together, you were going to write her a letter expressing your gratitude, what would you say?

PRESIDENT IKEDA: Now that's the toughest question you could have asked me! My wife is my dearest companion in life. She has been at times my nurse, my secretary, my mother, my sister, my daughter, and more than anything, my best and closest comrade in our struggle.

I don't really know what I'd say. If I were going to give her an award, I think it would be a "Smile Award." . . . My greatest hope is that we are both in good health to share our golden anniversary (in 2002). Please allow me to make the content of my letter of appreciation my homework, due on that day.[12]

In Life After Life

SASAKI: But the interviewer persisted. She begged you to say something, even if it was brief and simple. You thought for a moment and said:

Hmmm. My wife knows the truth about me better than anyone else, and I think that I know her devotion and patience better than anyone else could. My marriage to her has been one of the greatest joys of my life.

So I think I would have to say, "When we are reborn, in the next life and the one after that, for all eternity: please be there for me." But I suppose that's not a letter of appreciation—it's more like a job assignment![13]

PRESIDENT IKEDA: The interviewer was so persistent that finally she cornered me!

MATSUOKA: I remember that after your final dialogue together, Dr. Toynbee handed to one of your assistants a list of names he had prepared of people whom he hoped you would meet in the future and also pursue discussions with.

PRESIDENT IKEDA: That's right. He left the memo with my assistant, saying that he didn't wish to seem presumptuous or to put me under any obligation. I am still grateful for his consideration in giving me that kind memo.

SASAKI: One of those on Dr. Toynbee's list was Aurelio Peccei, cofounder and president of The Club of Rome. You first met him in Paris in 1975. It was May, when the first spring green had appeared, and you held your dialogue in the garden of the SGI community center in Paris.

PRESIDENT IKEDA: The revolutions that humanity has experienced up to now—the industrial revolution, the scientific revolution—have all been external revolutions. We both completely agreed that humanity's next revolution must be an inner revolution—the human revolution.

SASAKI: You met Dr. Peccei several times after that as well: in Tokyo, in Florence, and again in Paris. Dr. Peccei had just returned to his home in Rome from London the day before your Florence meeting, but he drove his car for four hours to be there.

PRESIDENT IKEDA: Yes, and he was seventy-two at the time. He had a very youthful spirit. All of the leading figures I have met seemed to grow younger as they aged, and they were able to throw themselves more energetically into their work in their later years. This is the mark of genuine greatness. It is important to maintain a vibrant, progressive spirit.

All too often people lose the drive to move ahead as they grow older. But the decision to draw back or to take a step forward hinges on only a slight difference in one's attitude or resolve. In the final chapter of our life, however, that slight difference can have momentous consequences.

CHAPTER 3

A Life of Commitment and Dedication

PRESIDENT IKEDA: On my sixtieth birthday (1988), Kono-suke Matsushita (1894–1989), the brilliant entrepreneur and founder of Matsushita Electric, sent me a letter of congratulations. It read in part: "Please regard today as the start of a period of even greater and more fulfilling activity. I pray that you will enjoy lasting good health and strive with the spirit of creating another Soka Gakkai all over again as you continue to devote yourself to world peace and the happiness and prosperity of all humanity."

At the time he wrote that, Mr. Matsushita was ninety-three. His frank good wishes struck a deep chord in me; I knew only too well the spirit in which they were written.

MATSUOKA: They are the words of a great pioneer. And they came true, didn't they? Through your tireless devotion to the development of the Soka Gakkai International, Nichiren Buddhism has now spread to some 128 countries and territories [192 as of November 2015], with members around the globe working for the happiness and prosperity of their local communities. Just as Mr. Matsushita said, you have created not only another, but an even larger, organization dedicated to peace, culture, and education.

SASAKI: When Austregésilo de Athayde (1898–1993), former president of the Brazilian Academy of Letters and one of the drafters of the Universal Declaration of Human Rights, met you for the first time [in February 1993], he was ninety-four years old, wasn't he?

PRESIDENT IKEDA: I was deeply humbled when I learned that this venerable champion of human rights had arrived at Rio de Janeiro's Galeão International Airport to wait for my arrival two hours before my flight was due. One of our SGI representatives had urged him to rest in a special waiting room, but he said with a smile: "I have been waiting for President Ikeda for ninety-four years. Another two hours is of no importance."

MATSUOKA: A *Seikyo Shimbun* photographer witnessed your first meeting with President Athayde and later described it to me. It was his first time to be assigned to cover one of your visits overseas, and there were no senior photographers with him at the airport, so he was very nervous in the presence of President Athayde. The Brazilian activist was physically frail and had been standing with the support of two assistants on either side of him, but the moment you arrived, President Athayde stood erect by himself and walked unaided to greet you. It was a very moving encounter. Fortunately, the photographer was able to capture that wonderful moment in a picture that later appeared in the *Seikyo Shimbun*.

PRESIDENT IKEDA: President Athayde had the demeanor of a magnificent old lion who had won many battles. In the course of his life, he wrote more than fifty thousand newspaper columns. He appeared on the radio weekly for thirty years and on television for twenty. And he also gave lectures on an almost weekly basis for some forty years.

While declaring "I have lived long enough, and so I have no fear of death," he also promised not to die before our

Austregésilo de Athayde, president of the Brazilian Academy of Letters, welcomes Mr. Ikeda at the Rio de Janeiro airport, February 1993.

dialogue was completed. He kept working on it until just a week before he was hospitalized for the last time. A little more than six months after our first meeting, I received the news that this great luminary in the struggle for human rights had passed away [on September 13, 1993]. Yet his fiery declarations of truth and justice still echo in my mind.

SASAKI: Many have read your dialogue, which was published under the title *Human Rights in the Twenty-first Century.*

MATSUOKA: Last month, the Brazilian Academy of Letters, of which you, President Ikeda, are a nonresident member, celebrated its centennial with much pomp and splendor at its former headquarters in Rio de Janeiro (July 1997). Soka Gakkai Vice President Hiromasa Ikeda attended the festivities on your behalf, and he had the opportunity to speak with Brazilian President Fernando Henrique Cardoso and many other distinguished guests on that occasion.

Fighting for the Causes of Freedom and Equality

PRESIDENT IKEDA: Next year I will be seventy. Compared to President Athayde's age when we met, I am still a youngster! I plan to keep exerting myself with boundless courage and vigor.

Nelson Mandela spent more than ten thousand days behind bars. When he was finally released from prison, he was over seventy, yet he continued his struggle to transform his country and took on the onerous responsibility of president of a new South Africa. I have met President Mandela. He is a man of great dignity, radiating the energy of one who has dedicated his life to the causes of freedom and equality.

MATSUOKA: When President Mandela came to Japan for the first time, he took time out of his busy schedule to meet with you at the *Seikyo Shimbun* head office in Tokyo (October 1990).

PRESIDENT IKEDA: My impression of him was as a towering and invincible warrior for human rights. A life dedicated to such noble ideals as his shines. When I think of the noble lives of our first two presidents, Tsunesaburo Makiguchi and Josei Toda, I cannot permit myself to stand still for even the briefest moment.

Mr. Makiguchi was fifty-seven when he encountered and embraced faith in Nichiren Buddhism. He later wrote of his tremendous emotion when he took that first great step: "With indescribable joy, I transformed the way I had lived my life for almost sixty years. The anxiety of searching in the dark for life's answers completely evaporated, and my inborn reserve and diffidence disappeared. My goals in life became increasingly grander and loftier, and my fears dwindled."[14]

Mr. Makiguchi was fifty-nine when he founded the Soka Kyoiku Gakkai (Value-Creating Education Society), the forerunner of the present Soka Gakkai, in November 1930. Today, someone that age would be on the verge of retirement. But what makes Mr. Makiguchi great is that at fifty-nine, he was just beginning!

From that time on, he held high the banner of value creation and fought for the happiness of the people and for a peaceful society. He remained committed to his lofty ideals until his death at age seventy-three in prison, where he had been confined by the agents of Japanese militarism.

The indestructible starting point of the Soka Gakkai was built by Mr. Makiguchi's unceasing struggle of his final years. He carried out the great undertaking that was his true purpose in life during the period we are calling the third stage of life.

SASAKI: We all know how, in his last letter from prison, Mr. Makiguchi wrote, "I am avidly reading the work of Kant."[15] To the last day of his life, he had a youthful spirit, dedicated to continual growth.

Progressing With Every Passing Day

PRESIDENT IKEDA: Mr. Toda once said that, before going to prison, the elderly Mr. Makiguchi was astonishingly active. He commented with real feeling that if a three-month interval went by between the time you'd last seen Mr. Makiguchi, you'd find that he hadn't been standing still, but had advanced three months ahead. Mr. Makiguchi's life was based on the spirit of true cause, of advancing from this moment on. He fought unceasingly without ever retreating a single step. Nor did this spirit change in the slightest under the harsh conditions of prison life.

MATSUOKA: Mr. Toda died at the age of fifty-eight, partly because his health was weakened by his nearly two years in prison.

PRESIDENT IKEDA: To us today, fifty-eight seems like a short lifetime. But brief as it may have been, in that time President Toda was able to secure the foundation for the entire future course of kosen-rufu. His life was one struggle after another, up to the very last. And just before his death, he held a ceremony [on March 16, 1958], to entrust the completion of his mission to the youth division. He gave his life to kosen-rufu, up to the moment of his death. He was truly majestic in his commitment.

To achieve our supreme goal in the end, as the culmination and completion of our life's work—this is the aim to which we should aspire in the third stage of our lives.

SASAKI: Your life has also been a constant struggle to advance, and then advance further still.

PRESIDENT IKEDA: Since becoming Mr. Toda's disciple fifty years ago, I have never rested from my labors for even a single day. Objectively speaking, in that half century, I could easily have collapsed at any time. I was fortunate enough to encounter Buddhism when I was nineteen, and then after Mr. Toda's death I devoted all my energies to carrying out the mission he bequeathed to me. My constitution was weak, and I had been told by my doctor that I would probably not live beyond thirty. The fact that I have been able to remain active over all these years is a result of the tremendous beneficial power of my faith and practice of Buddhism.

And it was precisely because I didn't think I had long to live that I tried to accomplish everything I had to each day, never putting anything off. Life's uncertainty motivated me in my pursuit of the goal of kosen-rufu.

Back in the fall of 1985, I went into the hospital for a period of ten days for a heart checkup. But even then, I continued to direct activities for kosen-rufu from my hospital bed. I deeply felt at that time that my hospitalization was a manifestation of Nichiren's great compassion. I was convinced that it happened in order to show me that the time had come to rise up once again and begin the true culmination of my life's work, and I was determined to work ten times, no, a hundred times harder than I had before.

Now was the time to say what had to be said. Now was the time to leave behind guidance on all subjects for later generations. And now was the time to thoroughly communicate to the world the truth about the Soka Gakkai and its wonderful significance and spirit. My feelings have not changed in the least to this very day.

MATSUOKA: We all see how selflessly you work day after day and the incredible struggle you are waging, and of course we worry for your health. I remember when you visited a forest in France's Loire region, and you took a deep breath of the air and said quietly to yourself: "What wonderful air! I know if I could stay here for just a little while, it would do wonders for my health. But I just can't. . . ."

PRESIDENT IKEDA: I'm afraid I just don't have the time for quiet recuperation. Anyway, my daily struggles for kosen-rufu have strengthened me physically, allowing me to enjoy good health. I am older than Mr. Toda was when he died. I passed the landmark age of sixty, and the third stage of my life is just beginning. I am prepared to keep on going, with the spirit that this is the most important period of my life.

As the lives of Mr. Makiguchi and Mr. Toda so eloquently illustrate, what matters is that we continue to develop an ever more expansive state of life and greater human brilliance with each passing year. That is the model for the third stage of life that they have left for us to follow.

SASAKI: Yes. Life is a continuing series of changes and more changes. If confronted with some momentous problem or crisis, we should look at it as an opportunity for a new start and continue to move forward. The important thing is to devote ourselves fully to the present and the future and to live a victorious life filled with the joy of mission and a sense of accomplishment.

MATSUOKA: In the course of our life, we will encounter many trials and challenges and also many crossroads. Our response and decisions at such times reveal our true mettle.

Trials Enrich Our Life

PRESIDENT IKEDA: If we triumph at a crucial moment, then in accord with the Buddhist principle of consistency from beginning to end, we will enter a sure path of victory in life. In fact, doing so determines whether or not we enter the path of good fortune and benefit throughout eternity. It all depends on our resolve and determination to emerge victorious. Nichiren writes, "The character *myo* [of Nam-myoho-renge-kyo] means to open" (WND-I, 145). Each time we face a trial in our lives, we must strive to further "open" and develop our state of life. By repeating that process through the years, we can experience an absolute and indestructible happiness.

The purpose of our lives, to the very last moment, is to achieve something of value. There is no life more noble than that of individuals who dedicate themselves to something they believe in and fight for it wholeheartedly; individuals who give their lives selflessly to their beliefs.

When you reach old age, you know in your heart if you are satisfied with your life or not. No one else can know this or decide it for you. The great challenge we face in our rapidly aging society is whether we can honestly say at the end of our days on this earth that our life was well spent.

CHAPTER 4

The Joy of Learning Throughout One's Life

SASAKI: This year [1997] again Soka University's Division of Correspondence Education held a special two-week, on-campus, summer course for its correspondence students. This program is now in its twenty-second year, and more than sixty-five thousand people have participated in it so far, traveling from all over Japan, from Hokkaido in the north to Okinawa in the south, and from as many as thirteen countries overseas.

PRESIDENT IKEDA: People who study while working, people who continue in the pursuit of learning no matter what their age are truly laudable. As university founder, I sent a message to the opening session of this year's course in which I said, "This alliance of people dedicated to learning that transcends the generations is spearheading the way toward a twenty-first century in which the third stage of life will be a period of boundless hope and fulfillment."

A number of years ago, I voiced a desire to enroll in a correspondence course at the university myself and study along with everyone else, but the university president refused to accept my application!

MATSUOKA: Of the approximately four thousand correspondent students enrolled at Soka University, nearly 10 percent—four hundred students—are over the age of fifty.

PRESIDENT IKEDA: That's wonderful.

SASAKI: In Japan, there are only fourteen universities, excluding the Open University of Japan,[16] that offer correspondence degree courses. Soka University's program is known for its very high graduation rate. A journalist who thoroughly investigated the Soka University program identified two reasons for this: the students' strong sense of purpose and a well-organized and administered study program.

PRESIDENT IKEDA: That is certainly most gratifying to hear. A fine tradition has been born and taken root at Soka University.

I have gone to observe some of the summer courses in years past. Not wanting to disturb the classes, however, I did so very unobtrusively, just looking into the classrooms from outside. I remember seeing a middle-aged man sitting near the Pond of Literature during the lunch break, lost in deep contemplation over some subject. It was beautiful to see someone engaged in such earnest pursuit of learning. A little distance away, near the pond's bridge, a number of other participants lay on benches catching forty winks—no doubt so that they would be refreshed for their next class. The whole scene was one of marvelous peace and tranquillity.

A summer program for correspondence school students at Soka University in Hachioji, Tokyo.

SASAKI: Yes, one often comes across scenes like that on the Soka University campus.

Learning Is Light and Ignorance Is Darkness

PRESIDENT IKEDA: I once presented the Division of Correspondence Education with a piece of calligraphy reading "the light of learning." I was inspired in my choice of words by one of founding Soka Gakkai President Tsunesaburo

Makiguchi's favorite sayings: "Learning is light and ignorance is darkness."

Everyone deserves the right to learn. Learning is a beautiful thing; it is light. Through learning, each of us creates a brilliant legacy of our youth, our studies, and our efforts that stays with us and enriches us forever.

SASAKI: The oldest correspondence student attending this year's summer course was Masanori Kitazume, seventy-eight, from Gumma Prefecture. When asked about his reason for enrolling in the correspondence degree program, he replied without hesitation: "For me, there is no tomorrow. There is only today. So I have to do it now. All President Ikeda's actions, too, are based on that spirit of no tomorrow."

PRESIDENT IKEDA: That's so great. I hope Mr. Kitazume will continue to do his best.

Incidentally, since the summer course takes place during the full-time students' summer holidays, some of the correspondence students stay in student dormitories on campus during the two-week course, don't they?

MATSUOKA: Yes. Takeshi Takahashi, seventy-seven, a victim of the Great Hanshin Earthquake,[17] was one of those who stayed in the dorms. The regular students had put up a poster in the dormitory's hallway that said, "Good Luck to

All the Correspondence Course Students!" Mr. Takahashi was deeply moved by this show of support, and he left a note on the pillow of the room in which he stayed. It said: "I will never forget this kindness as long as I live. I am only here for the special summer course, but I will continue to do my best. . . . I apologize that I can do no more to show my appreciation than to leave this memo." His wife, Asae, seventy-six, a retired nurse, accompanied him to Tokyo to support him in his studies during the course.

Mr. and Mrs. Takahashi have been living in prefabricated temporary housing for two years now after losing their home in the earthquake. Sharing with many others the pain and suffering of losing everything in that disaster, Mr. Takahashi decided to study for a law degree out of a wish to open a free legal counseling service in his area for those in need.

SASAKI: Mr. Takahashi has been a member of the men's division Kusunoki Chorus in Hyogo Prefecture for twenty-one years since its founding. He is also a past winner of Japan's public television station NHK's long-running amateur-talent show, *Nodo Jiman* (I'm Proud of My Voice).

One of our *Seikyo Shimbun* reporters who visited his home told me that Mr. Takahashi copies passages from Nichiren's writings and from your speeches almost every day, and he has pasted them all over the walls of his home, so there's not even room left to hang a calendar!

Mr. and Mrs. Takahashi's home, which they generously allow to be used as a base for Soka Gakkai district activities, is always filled with the warmth and laughter of high-spirited members.

PRESIDENT IKEDA: I wish to commend Mr. Takahashi on his vigorous efforts. President Makiguchi was a firm advocate of lifelong education. He himself began to study English after the age of fifty. And even in his sixties and seventies, he continued to learn with more energy and enthusiasm than most young people.

In the West, universities already play a leading role in providing adult and lifelong education. Universities of the Third Age, which began in France, are spreading in many countries, including the United Kingdom, the United States, Germany, Spain, and Canada.

SASAKI: Each year Soka University receives many letters from its correspondence students expressing appreciation for being offered a place where they can pursue their studies later in life.

PRESIDENT IKEDA: I'm happy that the correspondence courses have been received with such enthusiasm. From the time I began to formulate plans to establish Soka University, I wanted to include an active correspondence education division. The gates to Soka University will always be open to those, irrespective of age, who have a spirit of challenge and a desire to learn, including those who were unable to study in their youth for various reasons or circumstances.

MATSUOKA: I have personally seen how you always offer unstinting encouragement and words of support to those who keep advancing with a spirit of challenge, and especially to those who are forging ahead despite daunting obstacles of fate or unfavorable circumstances.

There were several students with hearing disability among those participating in the special summer session this year. Some of the regular day students who are proficient in sign language volunteered to serve as their interpreters, staying with them throughout the course to convey the content of the lectures and discussions to them.

This reminds me of the time you visited a school for the blind in India [in 1979].

PRESIDENT IKEDA: I was accompanied on that visit by Mr. K. R. Narayanan, who last month [July 1997] was elected as India's new president. He was then vice chancellor of New Delhi's Jawaharlal Nehru University, and we talked together at length.

The educational institute was attached to a fine comprehensive school in Narendrapur on the outskirts of Calcutta. The campus was shaded by huge green trees and graced with bright red bougainvillea blossoms. There were dormitories, spacious playing fields, and all kinds of garden plots and pens for domestic animals. It was a wonderful facility that provided education for students from elementary school through university level. The principal of the school was also blind. He showed me a manual training workshop where students were earnestly at work.

MATSUOKA: I remember that a group of the students brought you a bouquet of flowers. You embraced them and patted them affectionately on the shoulder to encourage them.

PRESIDENT IKEDA: Yes, I remember it well. Four students came to me with the bouquet.

MATSUOKA: You said to them in a resounding voice, "Despite the challenges you may face, I hope you will never forget to strive to live greater and greater lives, day after day!" You called out those words with boundless warmth and affection. You also told them: "We are all equal no matter who we are. What counts are the dreams you build for yourself and how bravely you strive to realize them. A person who does that can be said to have truly triumphed in life!" The students seemed to absorb your words with their entire beings. Bright smiles lit their faces at your encouragement.

Undefeated Even Facing a Death Sentence

SASAKI: Soka University has been able to develop its correspondence education to such an extent and lead the Japanese educational world because it was supported by such boundless love and commitment to the realization of each person's full potential.

I remember a quiet interlude on one of your overseas trips when you visited the residence of Beethoven in Vienna [in 1981]. You remarked to those accompanying you that despite the fact that fate had cruelly robbed one of the world's greatest musicians of his hearing—a fate equivalent to a death sentence for a musician—Beethoven was not destroyed by this loss.

PRESIDENT IKEDA: Beethoven himself declared: "I shall seize Fate by the throat, it shall never wholly subdue me. Oh, it is good to live one's life a thousand times!"[18] A person who triumphs over fate lives a life ten, a hundred, a thousand times more satisfying than one who succumbs to fate without a struggle. Such an individual grows more youthful and vigorous with each passing year.

SASAKI: So "it is the heart that is important." One of our readers, an elderly gentleman, writes: "Although I have been actively practicing Buddhism and participating in Soka Gakkai activities these many years, I feel as if I am slowly growing senile, and I am disturbed by this. What can I do?"

PRESIDENT IKEDA: The gentleman who wrote this letter and others who may share the same concern can, I think, take comfort in the fact that most people who are lucid enough to worry about whether they are growing senile are probably actually far from it. Essentially, I believe that our basic spirit as practitioners of Buddhism should be to never be perturbed by anything that may happen. People tend naturally to be pessimistic. I think it's important to make a conscious effort to look on the bright side.

This is a subject that I hope we can discuss in more detail in future installments, but the fundamental solution lies in faith and our Buddhist practice.

CHAPTER 5

Savoring the Sweetness of a Life Well Lived

MATSUOKA: Shinsaku Matsuura, a reporter for the *Sei-kyo Shimbun,* recently did a story on Kyokusui Yamazaki, the renowned *biwa* (Japanese lute) performer and composer who has been designated one of Japan's "living national treasures," the first *biwa* performer to be given this honor. Ms. Yamazaki, ninety-one, is a member of the Soka Gakkai Arts Division. Despite the unparalleled acclaim Ms. Yamazaki has achieved in her field, she continues to strive for perfection, "In art, you can never be satisfied," she says. "You have to keep learning until the day you die."

SASAKI: Ms. Yamazaki began learning the *biwa* when she was only eight years old, under a very strict teacher. By the time she was in her teens, she had made a name for herself as a talented performer on the Chikuzen *biwa*. She sparked great interest throughout Japan for this type of *biwa*, which until then had been popular in only one small region of Kyushu. Her achievements as a musician are incomparable.

Ms. Yamazaki triumphed over many personal difficulties in the course of her long and successful career. She waged a painful battle with rheumatism, which deformed her right hand—the one she used to hold the plectrum and strike the *biwa* strings. She also devotedly nursed her husband who suffered from a disability, becoming the sole breadwinner for her family.

PRESIDENT IKEDA: Yes, I have heard her story. I am so happy that she is still healthy and active today.[19]

MATSUOKA: Ms. Yamazaki's performances have been praised by knowledgeable critics as "shining like a jewel" and "a music illuminated by love." Some have even called her "a beacon for all those in the arts." When she performed at an Arts Division meeting in Tokyo in 1995, her performance was so powerful that a hushed, reverent silence fell over the auditorium. Members of the Arts Division declared that her supremely accomplished singing and playing had made them deeply reflect on their own art.

PRESIDENT IKEDA: I personally will never forget the moving rendition she once gave of "The Great Hero of Kusunoki" (Dainanko) in Kansai.

SASAKI: Ms. Yamazaki also singled out that occasion, calling it one of the most precious memories of her life. She said she would never forget how you came over to her after the performance to express your delight and appreciation and warmly embraced her.

When she has her *biwa* in hand, she is a very impressive presence, but members have remarked that at meetings, she sits with quiet dignity toward the back of the room and doesn't call attention to herself.

MATSUOKA: She's still very active, giving monthly lessons to her students, and she composes a new piece just about every year. She once remarked with a chuckle, "As I have aged, my voice has declined somewhat, but strangely enough I keep coming up with ideas for one new composition after another!"

Kyokusui Yamazaki, a Japanese national treasure.

SASAKI: One of her students said that he learns something new each time he hears her perform. He said: "Though she keeps saying she's gone as far as she can go, I'm sure she'll keep reaching new heights of creativity until the day she dies. If that wasn't the case, she wouldn't have all the students she has. Neither her technical skill nor her commitment to her art show the slightest sign of decline."

PRESIDENT IKEDA: The same was true of President Toda. To the very last, even on his deathbed, he urged us, his disciples, "You must never let up in your struggle against evil!" Having a great mentor is the greatest happiness one can experience in life.

MATSUOKA: I agree completely.

Apparently, the first thing on Ms. Yamazaki's agenda each morning is to pencil her eyebrows. She takes care of her appearance, so that she's always ready if a visitor arrives. She's still fully involved in life. Mr. Matsuura, our reporter, remarked that Ms. Yamazaki's skin was glowing and that she cut a strikingly handsome figure in a violet-colored kimono.

SASAKI: Ms. Yamazaki says that her most enjoyable hour of the day is when she shares a drink at dinner with her son and his family, with whom she now lives. She drinks two small glasses of beer, which tend to make her even more cheerful and talkative. And if there's a snack of her favorite fried chicken to go along with the beer, why, she's in seventh heaven!

PRESIDENT IKEDA: A happy family life certainly contributes to a long life. The role that family can play is great.

MATSUOKA: Ms. Yamazaki's granddaughter and disciple, Yoshie, says of her grandmother: "No matter how tired she is when she arrives home, she never neglects to chant. She reads the newspaper every day, always looking for any piece of guidance or article by President Ikeda. I learn a great deal from her honest and simple faith." Ms. Yamazaki proudly relates that she prays daily for the good health of you and Mrs. Ikeda and for the development of the art of *biwa* and the education of new young performers.

SASAKI: How wonderful! It would be ideal if everyone could continue, like Ms. Yamazaki, to pursue the challenge of striving for self-mastery and perfecting their craft or work until the very end, but it isn't easy, is it?

MATSUOKA: Our readers have questions relating to that issue. "I find it hard to fill my days," writes Nagamasa Ogasawara, eighty-three, from Hiroshima. Another reader, Masashi Shimmen, forty-six, from Kyoto, writes, "Why is it that as I grow older I have a harder time finding goals to strive for?"

In Old Age, You Can Bring Your Life
to a Satisfying Conclusion

IKEDA: I'm sure many people have encountered these same difficulties. They are emblematic of the problems we face today. Jonathan Swift (1667–1745), famous for his *Gulliver's Travels*, wrote in "Thoughts on Various Subjects," "Every man desires to live long; but no man would be old."[20] Certainly this statement can be interpreted in a variety of ways, but I tend to see it as a pointed warning. In other words, it's all very well to want to live long, but we shouldn't lose sight of what it is that we seek to gain by doing so.

MATSUOKA: Average life expectancy in Japan is at an all-time high. We have become a society of long life. Now we must decide how to spend those longer lives fruitfully. As we confront old age for a much longer period of time, we are forced to come to a new understanding of it. We need to build a society that genuinely celebrates old age and supports long and productive lives.

SASAKI: In general, people have a very negative attitude toward aging. Buddhism includes aging among the four sufferings—birth, aging, sickness, and death—and teaches that it is one of the fundamental causes of human suffering.

MATSUOKA: Yes. The very rationale of Buddhism is to conquer the sufferings of birth, aging, sickness, and death. This is symbolized by the story of Shakyamuni's first encounter with the four types of sufferings, which motivated him to give up his royal status, leave his palace, and seek enlightenment.

PRESIDENT IKEDA: As you have both said, the goal of Buddhism is to solve the problems of birth, aging, sickness, and death. But the heart of Nichiren Buddhism does not simply lie in transcending those four sufferings. In *The Record of the Orally Transmitted Teachings*, he states, "The words 'four sides' [of the Treasure Tower] stand for birth, aging, sickness, and death. We use the aspects of birth, aging, sickness, and death to adorn the towers that are our bodies" (OTT, 90). He thus elucidates a deeper understanding of those four sufferings, observing that they are transformed into treasures that add dignity and splendor to "the towers that are our bodies," to the Treasure Tower of life itself.

MATSUOKA: In other words, we possess within us the mystic power to transform an apparently negative phenomenon such as getting old into something positive.

PRESIDENT IKEDA: There is a saying that goes, "To a fool, old age is a bitter winter; to a sage, it is a golden time." Everything depends upon your attitude, how you approach life. Do you look at old age as a period of decline ending in death, or a period in which one has the opportunity to attain one's goals and bring one's life to a rewarding and satisfying completion? Is old age a descending path leading to oblivion or an ascending path taking one to new heights? The same period of old age, especially in terms of the richness and fulfillment you experience during those years, will be dramatically different depending upon your own outlook.

SASAKI: In a letter we received from Kazuko Umehara, sixty-seven, a reader from Kyoto, there was the following valuable suggestion: "I try to convince everyone I know to catch themselves in daily conversation whenever they are about to use some expression that negates their potential. We need to banish any expression of defeat from our minds—for example, statements or thoughts such as 'I can't do it,' 'I'm too old,' 'There's no point in my trying,' 'I'm past it,' or 'It's too hard.' Instead, we should be affirming what we can still do, the great promise that we still have, telling ourselves: 'I won't give up yet,' 'I'm still young,' 'I can still do it,' 'I've still got plenty of energy and vigor.' Just by changing the way we speak, we can change our pattern of behavior into a positive direction."

MATSUOKA: I feel more positive just listening to Mrs. Umehara's letter!

Living Out My Remaining Years in Idle Retirement Is Not For Me

PRESIDENT IKEDA: Nichiren describes the incredible difference that our fundamental approach to life can make. Discussing the secret and mystic expedient of the "Expedient Means" chapter of the Lotus Sutra, he says: "Secret means strict [or without a single exception]. The three thousand worlds, every single one of them, exist [in one's life]" (OTT, 22). There is a world of difference in how we refer to old age as well—whether we view it as the "remaining years of our life" or the "third stage of our life." "Remaining years" sounds like some useless leftover; the "third stage," however, emphasizes the shining potential life still holds for us.

The great German author and thinker Goethe writes: "Joy of existence is great, / Joy at existence is greater."[21] A life of purpose and commitment begins with setting goals for oneself. I will never forget what former President Fernando Belaúnde Terry of Peru once said to me when I visited his country.

SASAKI: That was when you were awarded the Order of the Sun of Peru in the Grade of Grand Cross [in March 1984], wasn't it?

PRESIDENT IKEDA: Yes, President Belaúnde was seventy-one at the time. He had been elected in the first democratic vote after Peru was restored to civilian rule, and he was deeply loved by the Peruvian people. "This is the last term I will serve as president," he said. "After that, I intend to devote my life to my field of specialty, architecture, to continue my studies, and to contribute to my nation and to humanity." President Belaúnde stated quite firmly, "Living out my remaining years in idle retirement is not for me. Because I am determined to live this precious life even more fully, I don't give the slightest thought to retirement."

MATSUOKA: SGI of Peru General Director Carlos K. Shima said that just recently Mr. Belaúnde viewed one of your photo anthologies and remarked as he did so: "I feel as if I am traveling around the world with President Ikeda. I will never forget our meeting."

SASAKI: You also visited Peru more than two decades ago [in March 1974], I remember. On that visit, you proposed an educational exchange program with the oldest university in Latin America, the National University of San Marcos. I can still see you standing out in the hot sun encouraging local SGI members who were working hard in their local communities. Because of your hectic schedule and the sweltering heat, you fell ill. The rector of the university, Dr. Juan de Dios Guevara Romero, paid a personal visit to your lodging to inquire after your health, as I recall. Over the years, you have contributed invaluably to friendly exchange between Peru and Japan.

MATSUOKA: Yes. Going back to what President Belaúnde said about not wanting an idle retirement but desiring instead to devote his entire life to serving humanity, I think that establishing a clear goal and then devoting your life to its realization is the best way to build a society in which long life is productive and contributes to the happiness of oneself and others alike.

PRESIDENT IKEDA: Founding Soka Gakkai President Tsunesaburo Makiguchi discussed the significance of establishing a purpose in life:

> Unless from the very start one first sets the highest goal for one's life, no matter how lofty and hard to realize it may seem, one's life will be filled with the anxiety that comes from searching futilely in the dark, and it will weave capriciously in one direction, then another, with no rhyme or reason.

The Lotus Sutra also says: "Our wish is that in future ages, we may use our long lives to save living beings" (LSOC, 280). This passage is a vow to live long in order to have more time to work to help other living beings.

The sweetness of a life well lived can be savored only when our life has a great purpose. That purpose, that goal, is our own. There is no need to compare ourselves to others. It is important to choose our own goal and to move forward toward achieving it in our own distinct way.

CHAPTER 6

Leading a Life of Purpose
and Commitment

PRESIDENT IKEDA: We agreed today to discuss the life of Mary H. Cornwall Legh (1857–1941), an Englishwoman who spent many years in Japan. There is a monument to Ms. Legh in a park near the Soka Gakkai's Many Treasures Center in the town of Kusatsu in Gumma Prefecture; her grave is also nearby. Local members have told me that she is still very deeply admired and respected by the people of Gumma.

SASAKI: She devoted her life to the care and treatment of people suffering from Hansen's disease, or leprosy.

PRESIDENT IKEDA: Yes. Mary Cornwall Legh was born into the British nobility, grew up on a large, wooded estate, and studied at university, receiving the highest education possible for a woman of her time. Then she abandoned her life of comfort to work as a Christian missionary in Japan.

SASAKI: Ms. Legh was born in 1857 in Canterbury, England. When she was young, she traveled around the world with her mother. After visiting North America and seeing Niagara Falls and many other sights, she came to Japan, where she was deeply impressed by the country's scenic beauty.

PRESIDENT IKEDA: After her mother's death, Ms. Legh returned to Japan alone at the age of fifty-one in 1908 to begin her missionary work. At fifty-nine, she decided to move to the Yunosawa area of Kusatsu in Gumma Prefecture and devote her life to the victims of Hansen's disease who had come to live there from throughout Japan.

MATSUOKA: The Yunosawa Hot Springs, located at the very lower reaches of the Yukawa River that flows through Kusatsu, became a kind of settlement for leprosy sufferers, who came seeking the beneficial medicinal effects of the waters that had a high sulfur content.

SASAKI: In those days in Japan, Hansen's disease was thought not only to be incurable but hereditary. [It carried great social stigma so that families of sufferers would usually try to conceal the presence of such an illness among one of their members.] Many victims came to live in this isolated community of fellow sufferers in Yunosawa [either voluntarily or because they had been cast out and had nowhere else to go.] Their lives were filled with great material hardship and emotional pain.

A Tiny Hut and Straw Boots

PRESIDENT IKEDA: Ms. Legh was a dedicated Christian, and she established medical and educational facilities for Hansen's disease patients and their children, giving her life to bring them security. She built several nursing and residential homes for patients. Eventually, she also built a clinic for them, where they could receive free medical treatment by a qualified doctor. She paid for all of these herself, using her enormous personal wealth. And what is really remarkable is that she began this great labor in the latter part of her life.

Ms. Legh lived very modestly. When her patients witnessed her humble and selfless way of life, they felt a surge of pride in enduring their own poverty.

SASAKI: During her weekly visits to give Bible instruction in Shimoma, some distance away from Yunosawa, Ms. Legh stayed overnight in a tiny makeshift hut without amenities of any kind. She was also known to be very kind not only to people but to animals as well.

PRESIDENT IKEDA: In winter, she wore the same straw boots as the local people and walked through the deep snows to visit the bedsides of the sick. Later, when rubber boots became available, she said she was happier about the invention of rubber boots than the light bulb, and she even used to wear those boots on her visits to Tokyo.

MATSUOKA: When other Westerners saw her poor attire and the humble circumstances in which she lived, they would exclaim in surprise that she lived like a beggar.

PRESIDENT IKEDA: Though she had been born and bred to the British upper classes, she was prepared to do anything to serve the people. She was a truly admirable person. She was able to do what she did because of her unselfish spirit. I think we can say that, at least in one respect, such a spirit of selflessness has contributed to the development of Christianity as a world religion. Similarly, it is precisely because SGI members have taken action for the betterment of society and the welfare of humanity, not seeking personal glory or gain for themselves nor abusing our organization, that the SGI has become a world presence too.

MATSUOKA: Taminosuke Nuki, who shared Ms. Legh's labors, wrote a book about her.[22]

PRESIDENT IKEDA: Yes, I read it too. He wrote: "Anyone observing the life of Ms. Legh could see that it transcended all logic and calculation. She had no hunger for worldly fame or fortune. She cared only for befriending, with justice and compassion, the sick whom the world had abandoned. She sacrificed herself. She labored endlessly. She spared no effort. She gave all her wealth to their encouragement and comfort."[23] How admirable!

SASAKI: Inspired by Ms. Legh, more than nine hundred people converted to Christianity. She personally washed and prepared for burial some three hundred of her converts—all sufferers of Hansen's disease—when they passed away.

PRESIDENT IKEDA: She was loved by all. They called her "Mom." For her seventy-seventh birthday, they made an album for her with that title. They dedicated it with profound gratitude to: "She who mothered us all, who had mothers once but lost them." It included the poems:

> *Though it is sad indeed*
> *To be ill*
> *But how fortunate we are*
> *To be blessed with*
> *Such a mother.*

★

> *Though she wears*
> *Only rough garments*
> *Our mother's*
> *Face shines*
> *With love.*[24]

How moving they are!

SASAKI: After her seventy-seventh birthday, Ms. Legh, who had been unflagging until then, began to show signs of deteriorating health, and eventually she moved to Akashi in Hyogo Prefecture to convalesce. She died at eighty-four on December 18, 1941, never once forgetting her beloved "family" in Kusatsu. At her request, her ashes were interred in the ossuary of the church at Kusatsu, along with those of many of her patients.

MATSUOKA: The Pacific War had just officially begun ten days before her death, and Japan and the United Kingdom had already severed diplomatic relations. The wartime slogan "The Americans and British Are Devils and Beasts" was on everyone's lips.

SASAKI: But the Japanese Minister of Health and Welfare sent a representative on his behalf to attend Ms. Legh's funeral. The next year, when the missionary's ashes were returned to Kusatsu and a ceremony conducted, a representative of the town's mayor as well as the chief of police and other local officials attended.

The Spirit of Devotion Is True Selflessness

PRESIDENT IKEDA: A memorial park was built on a hill overlooking Yunosawa, and a monument to Ms. Legh's life erected on it, indicating just how well-respected and loved she was, regardless of her nationality. Ms. Legh had a wonderful life, I am certain. She found a noble cause to devote herself to, took it up gladly and bravely, and gave everything to fulfilling her chosen vocation.

In Buddhism, a person's true greatness lies in their behavior, in how they have lived their life. It is important to develop a way of looking at the world and at people with unclouded eyes, with undistorted vision, transcending doctrine and orthodoxy. The ultimate measure of faith is in the spirit of devoting one's life, far surpassing any quest for personal merit. This spirit of devotion is true selflessness. It is to cast aside selfish desires. It is complete dedication to the Law and to humanity. The Soka Gakkai is what it is today precisely because its members have always acted with such a spirit of total commitment.

I will never forget those who have worked so hard alongside me to support the Soka Gakkai through the years. I am sure that Nichiren Daishonin also praises their tremendous efforts. Because they have worked so hard, I want all members from those early years to stride vigorously through their third stage of life and bring their lives to a wonderful completion.

MATSUOKA: You composed a *waka* poem to commemorate your fiftieth year since embracing faith:

> *For fifty years*
> *I have advanced with a spirit*
> *Of selfless devotion*

At last fulfilling
The vow I made for this lifetime

Reading it, I deeply felt that it is this spirit that is important.

PRESIDENT IKEDA: Just the other day [August 25, 1997], I met with Li Chengxian, widow of the late Chang Shuhong (1904–94), who was the director of the Dunhuang Relics Research Institute and custodian of the treasures of Dunhuang. Madame Li and her husband pledged together to devote their lives to preserving, studying, promoting, and passing on to the next generation the treasures of Dunhuang. They never gave up, in spite of the loneliness of the desert, the impoverished conditions in which they lived, the scorn of thoughtless people, and persecution by the authorities.

Madame Li has spent her life in selfless service to the art of Dunhuang by her own choosing. Even today the fires of creativity burn within her undiminished—she has recently embarked on a project to create new caves at Dunhuang for contemporary wall paintings. Her grand vision is to invite artists from around the world to participate in this project. She says she would like to build a modern-day version of the Mogao Caves and the Cave of the Thousand Buddhas in these years spanning the end of the twentieth and the beginning of the twenty-first century. At her advanced age, she still has glorious plans. I was deeply moved talking with her.

SASAKI: I know many may consider it rude to mention a woman's age, but Madame Li is seventy-two. She is still healthy and active. In the August meeting, she described her excitement at meeting you for the first time in Beijing seventeen years ago, saying that she could still see that moment clear as day.

PRESIDENT IKEDA: Yes, that was in April 1980 on my fifth visit to China. Sun Pinghua (1918–97), who was then president of the China-Japan Friendship Association, introduced me to her and her husband. On that trip, Deng Yingchao, the widow of the late Chinese Prime Minister Zhou Enlai, invited me to her home in Zhongnanhai, Beijing. I also had an opportunity to meet with many of China's new leaders, and I gave a commemorative lecture at Beijing University on the occasion of receiving an honorary doctorate from that institution.

MATSUOKA: I remember Sun Pinghua, who knew of your busy schedule, saying to you in his fluent Japanese: "There is someone I really think you should meet. He is a wonderful person. I know how busy you are, but please make just a little time. You will not regret it." He was referring to Chang Shuhong.

PRESIDENT IKEDA: Chang Shuhong and Madame Li came to my lodgings at the Beijing Hotel. The day before, the seventy-seven-year-old Mr. Chang had just returned from what was then West Germany. We had a very pleasant meeting and conversation that lasted two and a half hours. We talked about the Silk Road and Dunhuang to our hearts' content. I was deeply struck by his passion for and commitment to Dunhuang, which earned him the nickname "desert freak."

MATSUOKA: Mr. Chang's greeting upon his first meeting with you was very memorable: "This morning I heard on the radio that Madame Deng Yingchao met with you yesterday. I have heard your name many times in the past. I am so happy to have the opportunity to meet you today in person!"

SASAKI: Now, seventeen years after that first meeting, Madame Li relates, "I have met Mr. and Mrs. Ikeda many times over the years in China and Japan, and each time our friendship deepens."

I Want to Continue My Unfinished Work in the Next Lifetime

PRESIDENT IKEDA: In our published dialogue,[25] Mr. Chang related his fateful encounter with the art of Dunhuang in a book of photographic plates when he was a student in Paris. He shares how, after learning of the existence of such wonderful paintings in his own homeland, he returned to devote his life to preserving them for all humanity. In the years that followed, he met with much hardship and persecution, but still, in his last years, he said that he knew that he had not been mistaken in choosing the life he did. He never regretted it, he declared. This is the way we ought to live our lives.

SASAKI: A life dedicated to kosen-rufu is like that, isn't it?

PRESIDENT IKEDA: Yes. When I asked Mr. Chang what profession he would choose if he were to be reborn again as a human being, he replied, "If I really could be reborn as a human being, I would once more choose to be Chang Shuhong and finish the work I have started."

In terms of our mission as Bodhisattvas of the Earth, we who embrace the Mystic Law also dedicate our lives to an eternal mission that exists across the three existences—our mission to continue the great undertaking of kosen-rufu.

SASAKI: The beautiful ties of friendship between you and the Chinese couple reminds me of the magnificent oil painting of Chomolungma, or Mount Everest, that they painted together and presented to you a few years ago. This masterpiece now adorns the entrance hall of the Tokyo Makiguchi Memorial Hall.

MATSUOKA: Yes. I am sure it is the result of a warm friendship that grew from "making a little time."

PRESIDENT IKEDA: The life of each of us is like a canvas. What kind of picture do we paint there? We don't have to be a celebrity or a genius. What's important is to fill our canvas in our own style and to our own satisfaction, depicting the brilliant drama of a life devoted to our own individual mission, with all of our heart and being, up to the last moment.

CHAPTER 7

The Secret of Long Life

PRESIDENT IKEDA: There is a Buddhist scripture[26] in which Shakyamuni speaks of conquering "the three forms of pride"—the pride of youth, the pride of health, and the pride of life—in relation to the universal sufferings of aging, sickness, and death.

The Buddha points out that drunk with the pride of youth, people have an aversion to those bent with old age; drunk with the pride of health, people have an aversion to those suffering from illness or disease; drunk with the pride of life, people have an aversion to the dead. Reminiscing about his youth, an elderly Shakyamuni remarks that he shed these three forms of pride. This event is related to the famous "four meetings"[27] and was a reason for his leaving home to seek enlightenment.

SASAKI: It is amazing that Shakyamuni was able to rid himself of these three forms of pride when he still enjoyed the privileged life of a prince.

PRESIDENT IKEDA: Yes, what sets him apart is that he turned his thoughts to the aging, the ill, and the dying at a time when he was at the very peak of his youth, in vigorous health, and filled with the joy of living.

It is important for us to remember that these three forms of pride that Shakyamuni identified are not just relics from the past that have no relevance to the present. Today in Japan in particular, we are facing the reality of a rapidly aging society, and there is much discussion of the changes we must make in terms of our social systems and institutions to respond to this new situation. Such discussions are of course important, but I believe we must also focus on the more essential issue of the mental pride or arrogance that has taken root in people's hearts and try to change human beings themselves.

MATSUOKA: That is so true.

PRESIDENT IKEDA: All too often people tend to despise and dislike that which is different from them. In my lecture at Harvard University [in September 1993],[28] I called this "an unreasoning emphasis on difference." Shakyamuni described this as "a single, invisible arrow piercing the hearts of the people."[29] By placing an unreasonable emphasis on difference, we set boundaries on our own lives and block ourselves off from wider possibilities. By fearing and rejecting what is different, we restrict ourselves to what we are now and shut the door on further growth and spiritual enrichment.

As long as people today continue to avert their gaze from the realities of aging, sickness, and death, they are denying their own future, rejecting their inevitable fate—for all of us, without exception, will experience these things.

MATSUOKA: People seem to regard aging as a negative thing, but I think there are many wonderful, beautiful, and positive things about growing old.

PRESIDENT IKEDA: We need to change our values, the way we look at aging. The rich fund of life experience that an older person has is a precious and irreplaceable resource, not only for the individual but also for those around him or her, and for society at large.

In one of his writings, Nichiren recounts how King Wen of the Chou dynasty in ancient China valued the elderly and respected their wisdom (see WND-1, 916). He goes on to say that the Chou dynasty lasted eight hundred years because of the wise policies of King Wen.

You can start from what you can put into practice immediately, such as sharing a few warm, heartfelt words with the elderly people around you. Let's work to promote concern and respect for the aged.

SASAKI: Yes. And as in all things, it starts with our own actions.

PRESIDENT IKEDA: Many times, the words of older people, based on their long and abundant experience, possess a wisdom and weight that can take your breath away. I know countless elderly people whose lives shine beautifully. People who have built an indestructible self through their work for kosen-rufu literally sparkle. The secret is to live with dignity and confidence.

At Ninety-Eight, She Began Lecturing at an Academy

MATSUOKA: I recently met a person who is a perfect example of that: Yoshi Takahashi, whom you introduced in your collection of essays *Haha no uta* (Ode to Mothers).[30] She is 103 years old. The day I visited her at her home in Fujisawa City, Kanagawa Prefecture, just happened to be her birthday. Her house was filled with flowers she had received from her grandchildren and her neighbors and friends, and she was as hale and hearty as ever.

PRESIDENT IKEDA: Yes, I know her well. At age ninety-eight, she became a special lecturer at an academy for training fashion coordinators! Until last year—that is, for five years, until she was 102—she lectured the young students at the school, and she was very popular. She made appearances on television, radio, and the lecture circuit, where she delivered wonderful speeches and responded to interview questions. It makes me so happy to know that she has remained active all these years.

SASAKI: I remember seeing her by chance on a television show. The interviewer was moved to tears by some of the accounts of her life that Mrs. Takahashi shared. Mrs. Takahashi emphasized the importance of courage, perseverance, and effort, and she said that she intended to keep going and live to see a peaceful twenty-first century. She spoke with impressive force and clarity.

PRESIDENT IKEDA: That's wonderful. Nothing brings me greater joy than knowing that the members who have been with us since the early days of our movement are living long and healthy lives, enjoying a fulfilling third stage of life.

MATSUOKA: Mrs. Takahashi gets up at five o'clock every day and starts the day off with gongyo and an hour of chanting. She says that every day she prays for the good health and longevity of you and Mrs. Ikeda, and for you, President Ikeda, to continue encouraging members around the world. She adds that she has every intention of ushering in the twenty-first century with you. Mrs. Takahashi remarked that since she has had the fortune to be born as a human being, it is her mission to work for the happiness and welfare of people in society.

Keep Looking Ahead and Advance With a Positive Spirit

PRESIDENT IKEDA: I have heard that she really looks forward to attending the monthly discussion meetings with members of her local organization, and that she writes a short poem for each meeting.

MATSUOKA: Yes. For the May meeting this year, she wrote:

> *How happy I am*
> *To celebrate May 3!*
> *At one hundred and three,*
> *Still healthy,*
> *Following the path of mentor and disciple.*

Mrs. Takahashi also talks to the plants in her garden as she tends them, and sometimes those words take shape as poems as well. For example:

> *As I speak*
> *To these silent*
> *Flowers*
> *I count the buds*
> *Of tomorrow's blossoms.*

Mrs. Takahashi also reads the *Seikyo Shimbun* every day, using a magnifying glass to read the print.

PRESIDENT IKEDA: What an excellent example for us all! It is women such as Mrs. Takahashi who have supported the Soka Gakkai, and indeed society, over the years.

SASAKI: A week after joining the Soka Gakkai, Mrs. Takahashi was in the audience at Yokohama's Mitsuzawa Stadium when Mr. Toda delivered his 1957 declaration calling for the abolition of all nuclear weapons. Her life has spanned the twentieth century. As one who remembers the songs that were popular during the time of the Sino-Japanese War (1894–95), the Russo-Japanese War (1904–05), and World War II, she states unequivocally, in a firm and resounding voice: "In war, so many bright young people are sacrificed in their prime. It is a terrible waste of life. Nothing is more terrible than war."

PRESIDENT IKEDA: Mrs. Takahashi was over sixty when she found faith in the Nichiren Buddhism and joined the Soka Gakkai, wasn't she?

MATSUOKA: Yes. She was sixty-three. At the time, she wasn't feeling well. Her heart was weak, and she frequently had dizzy spells and fainted. She joined because she wanted to improve her health. She says she finds it amazing that her wish was so completely realized and that she's been able to live to over one hundred.

PRESIDENT IKEDA: It's the principle of "faith extending life" in action. I once presented her with a cane along with a message that I was praying for her to continue enjoying a long and fulfilling life.

SASAKI: Yes, and she regards that cane as a precious treasure. She says that when she picks it up each morning, she feels like she is starting the day with a handshake from you.

PRESIDENT IKEDA: I think the secret of long life can be found in the following words of Mrs. Takahashi: "There's nothing to fret or worry about. Brooding over problems serves no purpose. You mustn't keep looking back and making comparisons with what happened in the past, letting it stop you from moving forward. You'll live a long time if you keep looking ahead and advancing with a positive attitude. You need to keep a positive outlook. And never grumble and gripe." This is an excellent attitude.

Does Mrs. Takahashi come from a long-lived family, by the way?

SASAKI: Actually, her father died at thirty-three and her mother lived only to be fifty-four, so we can't really say that she comes from a family that is particularly long lived. I think this shows, however, that attitude and lifestyle are very important factors in achieving a long life.

PRESIDENT IKEDA: Ihsan Dogramaci (1915–), the famous Turkish pediatrician and educator with whom I conducted a dialogue [in 1992], said that he believes the secret to a long life is "a peaceful heart."

MATSUOKA: Yes. I still remember him declaring that with a peaceful heart such as yours, you should live to more than a thousand years!

PRESIDENT IKEDA: Actually, I think his sharp wit is the secret to his own long life.

A Happy Life Is a Healthy Life

MATSUOKA: It's said that many people get sick at the change of the seasons. Let's talk a while about things that elderly people should look out for at such times.

PRESIDENT IKEDA: One of the most important things is to avoid overexertion. Exhaustion is the cause of many, many illnesses. If you want to live long, it's important to get enough rest. Attention should also be paid to diet, with care being taken to ensure that meals are nutritionally well balanced and to refrain from eating late at night.

There is a saying, "Laughter makes young; anger makes old." Laughter and a sense of humor play an important part in staying in good health. If you look on the bright side of things and act positively, you'll have a cheerful and happy life. And a happy life is a healthy life.

SASAKI: In the discussion series "A New Century of Health: Buddhism and the Art of Medicine" featured in the *Seikyo*

Shimbun,[31] you spoke with various experts—representatives of the Soka Gakkai doctors' division and nurses' group—about ways to prevent senility. Would you mind summing up the key points here again for our readers?

PRESIDENT IKEDA: Certainly. The best ways to stimulate the brain, and thus prevent the onset of senility, it seems, are to use our hands and feet, and to interact with others. Some even call our hands a "second brain." Writing letters or performing some other activity that requires manual dexterity stimulates the brain cells.

When we perform morning and evening gongyo, we join our palms together in prayer. The very act of joining our palms together creates a moderate tension in the muscles of our hands and fingers, which is said to provide the brain with excellent stimulation.

MATSUOKA: Mrs. Takahashi says that she still enjoys working in the kitchen and preparing food. At 103, she's still using her hands. She showed them to me, as a matter of fact, and they are very pretty hands, smooth and soft.

SASAKI: Walking is another excellent way to prevent senility.

PRESIDENT IKEDA: That's right. Using one's voice, as in singing, and moderate exercise are also crucial in preventing senility. It's important to keep in mind that elderly people tend to be especially susceptible to sudden changes in their environment and to strong stress, often with adverse consequences for their health and well-being. We should strive to create environments for them in which they feel relaxed and at ease.

SASAKI: Apparently, people with the following characteristics run a higher risk of becoming senile: (1) stubborn and selfish people; (2) short-tempered people; (3) people with few friends; (4) people without a sense of humor; (5) people who are obsessed with money and possessions and who don't trust others.

PRESIDENT IKEDA: We should all watch out for those traits in ourselves.

In contrast, it's been said, too, that people who have a strong sense of purpose, a sense of responsibility, who work hard to achieve a goal, are less likely to become senile.

SASAKI: In the art of medicine discussion, you also suggested four mottoes for a healthy life, didn't you?

PRESIDENT IKEDA: Medically speaking, proper diet, sufficient exercise and sleep, and the reduction of stress are regarded as the keys to good health. All of these factors are incorporated in my four-point motto:
(1) "Do an invigorating gongyo";
(2) "Conduct your daily life in a reasonable and productive manner";

(3) "Be of service to others"; and

(4) "Maintain sound eating habits."

I am always praying for the health and long life of our members who work so hard day and night for kosen-rufu.

CHAPTER 8

A Gift From Parents

PRESIDENT IKEDA: We've received many letters from readers regarding long life.

MATSUOKA: Yes. Let me read a bit from a letter from Mr. Toshio Takahashi, a seventy-seven-year-old barber living in Tochigi Prefecture.

Barbers work with their hands and have to concentrate. In our conversations with customers while we are working, we also get glimpses into other lives, which is always stimulating. In the nearly five hundred barbershops in Utsunomiya City, fewer than ten elderly barbers have shown any symptoms of senility. I am very grateful that I chose this profession, and every day during my morning and evening prayers I thank my parents, who were also barbers.

SASAKI: Last year Mr. and Mrs. Takahashi celebrated their golden wedding anniversary. They are both still happily working, and they are also active in the Soka Gakkai, with Mr. Takahashi serving as a vice chapter chief.

PRESIDENT IKEDA: What an encouraging example. I have heard that the barber's profession and the art of medicine are closely linked. Long ago, barbers actually served as surgeons. The twisting red, white, and blue-striped barber pole symbolizes the arteries (red), veins (blue), and bandages (white). Both doctors and barbers also wear white robes.

I'm sure that the concentration that the barber's profession demands has helped Mr. Takahashi stay healthy and active to such a wonderful age.

MATSUOKA: The need to stay alert and to concentrate does keep people young.

PRESIDENT IKEDA: Shuhei Morita, the Soka Gakkai doctors' division leader, once remarked to me when he was head of surgery at the Yokohama Red Cross Hospital, that he never felt tired when he was performing surgery, even though he might be on his feet in the operating room for eleven hours straight. But one hour on a crowded train doing nothing but hanging onto the hand strap, he noted, exhausted him. I think this is a perfect example of the way that serious engagement in some kind of focused task can tap unlimited reserves of hidden potential in us.

SASAKI: The more we make use of our abilities, the more we can develop and hone them.

PRESIDENT IKEDA: A noted American gerontologist, Belle Boone Beard (1898–1984), spent two decades studying centenarians. She concluded from her research that when people continuously make use of their powers of memory and concentration, those abilities do not decline—in other words, "Memory shows no upper age limit."[32]

MATSUOKA: Speaking of memory, I am always astounded by yours. You remember things about others that happened twenty or thirty years ago with incredible clarity. People are always amazed how vividly you manage to recall things that even they had long forgotten or, on occasion, hoped you wouldn't remember!

SASAKI: You have written tens of thousands of poems to encourage and inspire members. Of course, I am astonished that you are able to produce such moving and beautiful poetry on the spur of the moment. But I am even more surprised how, for example, you'll often suddenly mention that you want to change a word or phrase in a poem you had written a week prior, and you still recall it perfectly, without any notes or memos.

MATSUOKA: SGI members are always at work somewhere around the world, and as the president of the SGI, you never have a moment's rest. Yet even in the midst of that incredibly busy schedule, you somehow find the time and the mental energy to be thinking about a poem you have sent to a friend. It's truly staggering.

I Concentrate My Entire Being in Each Moment of Each Encounter

PRESIDENT IKEDA: It's one thing to know, on an intellectual level, that each moment of your life may be the last. But it's much harder to actually live and act, on a practical level, based on that belief. I have lived these last fifty years of my life with an absolute determination to triumph in life. Whenever I meet with one of our members, I try to extend myself to them to the utmost, for that may be our last encounter. I never leave room for regret. That is why each meeting I have with others remains vivid and fresh in my mind forever, transcending the passing of the years. I concentrate my entire being, an eternity of thought and feeling, in each moment of each encounter.

SASAKI: I am impressed by the seriousness with which you regard even the briefest encounter. The challenge we face is to take this limited span of years we have and, instilled with hope and optimism, try to do the very best we can.

PRESIDENT IKEDA: Norman Cousins, the "conscience of America," with whom I conducted a dialogue, declared that hope was his secret weapon. "Death is not the ultimate tragedy in life. The ultimate tragedy is to die without discovering the possibilities of full growth," he said.

And he also said: "Death is not the greatest loss in life. The greatest loss is what dies within us while we live."

MATSUOKA: No matter how old we are, we must never lose the spirit of rising to a challenge.

Enveloped in the Beautiful Green Cloak of Spring at Moscow State University

PRESIDENT IKEDA: When Anatoly Logunov, the Russian nuclear physicist and director of the Institute of High-Energy Physics, was rector of Moscow State University, we spoke together about the way his own family had evolved over the years. According to Dr. Logunov, his family changed as his children grew older. When his son and daughter had become adults, Mr. Logunov and his wife enjoyed what he called "a second youth." Then, after reaching the age of fifty, they experienced "a third youth." He wanted to make the point that our lives are never static; we are always changing, and we must always continue to pursue self-development and self-improvement.

SASAKI: When you began your dialogue with Dr. Logunov, in the dignified atmosphere of the rector's office, Moscow State University was enveloped in the beautiful green cloak of spring. It was May 1981.

PRESIDENT IKEDA: A large tapestry that had been presented by Beijing University to commemorate Moscow State University's bicentennial adorned one wall of the rector's office. Depicting the Moscow State University campus in its entirety, the tapestry remained in place there even during the height of political tension between the Soviet Union and the People's Republic of China. This was a wonderful sight, I thought, and a fine example of the way in which the world of learning transcends political conflict.

MATSUOKA: It's interesting that Dr. Logunov used the expression *third youth*.

PRESIDENT IKEDA: Yes. I hope that everyone can experience a third stage of life that is like a "third youth." Youth is not something that fades with age. Our attitude toward life is what makes us young. As long as we have a forward-looking, positive attitude and spirit of challenge, we will gain depth as people and our lives will shine with a brilliance that is ours alone.

Dr. Logunov quoted the lines of the Russian poet Aleksandr A. Blok, "And endless battle! We only dream of peace,"[33] adding the personal insight that "life is good to those who are dynamic, sensitive to the pulse of the times, and who make an effort to align their lives with its rhythms." Life itself is the greatest ally of those who make the later years of their lives a "third youth."

Mr. Ikeda meets with Rector Anatoly Logunov (left) of Moscow State University during the SGI president's third visit to the then-Soviet Union, May 1981.

SASAKI: The day before meeting with Dr. Logunov [in May 1981], you visited Lyudmila Gvishiani, the late Soviet Premier Aleksey N. Kosygin's daughter and director of the National Library of Foreign Literature in Moscow. I remember that occasion very well.

PRESIDENT IKEDA: Ms. Gvishiani waited for me at the entrance of the National Library. I was immediately reminded of her late father; she had the same wise, clear blue eyes. She was a fine woman with a distinct air of intelligence and refinement.

SASAKI: She recalled that after returning home from work one day, her father had exclaimed to his family: "Today, I met an extraordinary and extremely interesting Japanese. Though we touched upon very complex issues, I was happy that our discussion was most satisfying." He was speaking of his first encounter with you on the occasion of your first visit to the Soviet Union in September 1974.

MATSUOKA: Ms. Gvishiani also said that these words made a special impression on her, because her father rarely spoke to his family about his work.

SASAKI: Yes. Ms. Gvishiani said she deeply appreciated your expression of condolences upon the death of her father, your visit, and your conversation with her. She remarked that she and her family had decided that they wished to present you with some mementos of her late father.

PRESIDENT IKEDA: She presented me with a cherished crystal vase engraved with her father's portrait that had been bestowed on him at the age of sixty upon receiving the high Soviet honor of "Hero of Socialist Labor." She also presented me with two leather-bound books, his last works, which lay in his private library up to the moment of his death.

"The warmth of my father's hands still clings to them. I offer them to you in his stead," she said, her eyes filling with tears.

SASAKI: Yes. It was such a moving moment that even the interpreter was overcome with emotion. With her gaze cast down, Ms. Gvishiani went on to say that she regarded her father as a true friend, and every day as the sun set, she felt a strong sense of his loss. You comforted her, saying that her father lived on in her heart, and she nodded silently in agreement.

MATSUOKA: In one corner of the National Library of Foreign Literature was a large "Soka Gakkai corner" filled with your books. Ms. Gvishiani was deeply attached to her father, and I know that she found her meeting with you, who had engaged in such fulfilling and warm human communication with her father, unforgettable.

The Example of the Deceased Encourages Those Who Survive

PRESIDENT IKEDA: The bonds of parent and child are strong, and a parent's way of life is deeply engraved on the child. I think we can say that one of the most important aims of our third stage of life is to be true to ourselves to the very last, becoming an inspiration to those around us. The memories a person leaves behind, the example he or she has set, can be a great source of encouragement and strength to those who survive.

MATSUOKA: A forty-nine-year-old member of the men's division has sent us a letter about his father, eighty, and his mother, seventy-nine, who live in Nagano city and who have dedicated their lives to the Soka Gakkai movement. He said he eventually became aware of the nobility of his parents' lives and is grateful for the example they have provided him. His father is a vice chapter leader and his mother is a vice district women's leader. He himself is also actively involved in the forefront of Soka Gakkai activities.

It's a wonderful letter that brings up many stimulating points, and I would like to introduce it to our readers. *(The letter appears below with the author's permission.)*

PRESIDENT IKEDA: It is fathers and mothers such as they who have built the Soka Gakkai. I am always praying for their happiness and well-being.

What can we contribute, what can we leave as a legacy for others in our third stage of life? After all is stripped away—our wealth, our fame, our social status—the one thing that remains after our death is the example of a life lived with purpose, dedication, and dignity.

A LETTER FROM A READER

Reading this series on the third stage of life, I decided to look back over the lives of my parents. My father is eighty and my mother is seventy-nine. Since finding faith in the teachings of Nichiren Daishonin in 1959, they have completely dedicated their lives to it. My father doesn't drink or gamble. The only things I can remember my father doing are reading the *Seikyo Shimbun* or Nichiren's writings, going out to spread Nichiren's teachings, and sitting before the Gohonzon and chanting. He has always been completely devoted to his faith and never indulged in personal pleasures or hobbies. When I was young I used to think his life was very dull.

But later I came to realize just how wrong I was.

At one time in my life, I had taken a wrong turn. I am sure that both my father and mother were deeply troubled as they watched me; I'm sure I made them weep in their hearts. But my father only said one thing to me, "You have given me the opportunity to chant Nam-myoho-renge-kyo. . . ." I felt an inexpressible shock at his words, and I couldn't understand why he thought as he did.

Today I walk forward, looking fondly at the example of my parents, ahead of me on the road of life. Neither of them seem old to me at all. They have the strength of people who have always fought for their cherished beliefs. Having dedicated their lives to kosen-rufu within the Soka Gakkai, they are not spending these last years of their lives helpless and dependent on others; they are still fighting and living their third stage of life to the fullest.

CHAPTER 9

Work Is the Key to Health

MATSUOKA: Recently, one of our readers sent us some materials he had collected on the factors that are believed to be responsible for the long life spans of people who live in Okinawa.

PRESIDENT IKEDA: Yes, Okinawa has the longest average life expectancy in Japan, doesn't it? And since Japan has the longest average life expectancy in the world, the longest within Japan means the longest in the entire world.

I first visited Okinawa just two months after I became the third president of Soka Gakkai on May 3, 1960.

SASAKI: The day you arrived in Okinawa, July 16, was the seven hundredth anniversary of the date on which Nichiren Daishonin submitted his treatise "On Establishing the Correct Teaching for the Peace of the Land" to Japan's rulers to remonstrate with them for their support of erroneous teachings.

MATSUOKA: At the recent World Peace Youth Culture Festival held in Hong Kong (February 1997), twenty members of the Okinawa young men's division represented Japan at the festival, performing the traditional Okinawan dance, the Kachashi, to great acclaim.

PRESIDENT IKEDA: Yes, that's right. The performance of the Hong Kong members and the traditional drum-and-dance performance of the South Korean members were also spectacular, but the Okinawan dance really stole the show. Okinawa has an international atmosphere. It is located at a key point along the maritime Silk Road, which has made it a melting pot of Asian culture.

SASAKI: The festival was held in the Hong Kong Convention and Exhibition Center, where the ceremonies for Hong Kong's return to China were later held. After the festival was over, and you and your guests had retired, Mr. Matsuoka and I remained. When your message declaring the festival a great success was conveyed to the participants in English and Cantonese, a great roar of joy went up throughout the hall.

PRESIDENT IKEDA: The term *Kachashi* means "to mix." The dance remains firmly rooted in daily Okinawan life, and it is performed regularly at all kinds of parties and gatherings. Everyone just gets in a circle and dances. There are no fixed steps; each person just improvises as he or she steps into the dancing ring.

Matsuoka: The youth division members from Okinawa visited the Hong Kong Soka Kindergarten with a group of SGI members from all parts of the world before the festival began. They lost no time in teaching the eager kindergarten students to dance, and the Kachashi dance wound its way from classroom to classroom, picking up more dancers along the way.

President Ikeda: Once you start dancing, all the barriers of age, gender, nationality, and race, melt away. Dance is a great equalizer. That equality is the spirit of Okinawa, a spirit that we can also see in the way in which the elderly are treated with love and respect there.

At the festival, our friends from around the world found themselves captivated by that Okinawan rhythm and joined together as one. The barriers between audience and performers disappeared.

Sasaki: Hifumi Kinjo, a young men's vice headquarters leader, played the *shamisen* (a traditional Japanese three-stringed instrument) for the dance. The Okinawan word for "sun" is *tida*. Mr. Kinjo and his friends have formed a pop group they call Tida Company, which uses traditional Okinawan instruments and musical influences in their songs and is very popular locally. They appear on television and have many fans.

PRESIDENT IKEDA: I'm so happy that they're doing well. Mr. Kinjo also performed at the 1994 Asia Youth Peace Music Festival held at the Fukuoka Dome in Kyushu, Japan, and he drew enthusiastic applause.

SASAKI: Yes. His mother, Hideko, is eighty years old. She has two older sisters, Toyo Kohagura, ninety-six, and Tooyo Oshiro, ninety-three.

MATSUOKA: All three of these long-lived sisters first encountered Buddhism and joined the Soka Gakkai during the great wave of propagation that took place around the time of your first visit to Okinawa.

SASAKI: Ninety-six-year-old Toyo Kohagura is now in a nursing home, but she is healthy and every day she reads the *Seikyo Shimbun*, from cover to cover, without glasses. Her ninety-three-year-old sister rises every morning at five. After taking care of her housework, she goes out to work in the fields. Her daughter, who lives with her, tries to stop her, but she says: "It's no fun sitting in the house watching TV with the fan on. I'd rather be out weeding."

PRESIDENT IKEDA: The Roman philosopher Seneca once said that work is the finest nutrition of the spirit, and that is very true. It's well known that many people age very quickly after they retire and lose the excitement and interest that work provided them. Most of Okinawa's elderly citizens are hard workers. It is also the local custom to treat elderly people well, and they have a distinct role in society. That is wonderful. Having a place to work and be productive contributes greatly to their health.

MATSUOKA: Whenever I report on elderly people, I am struck by the strength they have. It is a strength that has allowed them to survive the hardships of war and poverty, an invincible spirit that I don't find in Japanese people born after World War II.

PRESIDENT IKEDA: Yes, I think that's true. Okinawa in particular suffered in World War II. It was the only part of Japan in which a ground war was fought, and the islands were struck with an onslaught of bombing so fierce it was called the "typhoon of steel." The attack changed the island's topography, blasting away mountains and valleys, and killed many innocent civilians.

Today's elderly residents of Okinawa are people who rose from the ashes of that devastated land. Okinawa was not rebuilt by the government or the military. It was rebuilt by the Okinawan people. This effort to rebuild was a true battle, and that no doubt is what instilled in the depths of their hearts the keen awareness of the meaning and nobility of life and of work.

SASAKI: The younger brother of Hideko Kinjo, feeling it would be unpatriotic to do otherwise, joined the army and was killed when still in his teens.

MATSUOKA: The Okinawans experienced the terrible inhumanity of the Japanese forces fighting on their islands, and they also always had a deep suspicion of mainland Japan. In the early days of the Soka Gakkai's activities on Okinawa, those who accepted faith in Nichiren's teachings were often ostracized for "worshiping mainland gods."

Living Out Our Lives Fully Is What Our Activities for Kosen-rufu Are All About

SASAKI: Tooyo Oshiro was the first member to embrace faith in Nichiren Buddhism in her region. Her two sisters followed suit and all three have lived long lives devoted to their faith.

PRESIDENT IKEDA: Their long lives are a demonstration of the greatness of Buddhism. Living out our lives fully and surviving the vicissitudes of life is what faith and what our activities for kosen-rufu are all about. These noble sisters of Okinawa have fought alongside me over the years, praying for the happiness of their friends, when many still derided the Soka Gakkai as a gathering of the sick and the poor. Without a doubt, they are advancing on the path of eternal good fortune and benefit.

SASAKI: Shortly before the Vietnam War, Hideko Kinjo was very, very poor—so poor that she honestly didn't know where her family's next meal would come from. She made necklaces out of shells she picked up on the beach and walked to the town of Kincho to sell them to American soldiers.

When she found she was pregnant with her sixth child, she seriously considered having an abortion. But a friend said to her, "You don't know what great mission this child might have." These words touched a core deep inside and, weeping, she offered prayers of apology and gratitude to the Gohonzon. That child turned out to be Hifumi Kinjo, who performed at the culture festival.

MATSUOKA: When he was a child, Hifumi and his family were laughed at because they lived in a house missing half its roof. But four years ago he managed to build a new, three-story house for his mother. The second floor of the house is used as the central Soka Gakkai meeting place for members of Onna Chapter's Tancha District, and they have had the concrete wall surrounding the water tank on the roof painted in pastel shades of the SGI tricolor flag—blue, red, and yellow. Against the deep blue tropical skies it is a sign that shouts out "Here's the Soka Gakkai!"

SASAKI: The Okinawa Training Center, a fortress of peace built on the site of an old nuclear missile launching pad, is located in the same district. The area where the three sisters worked so hard for kosen-rufu has now been transformed into a region of peace and prosperity that is visited by SGI members from all around the world.

Those Who Suffer the Most Should Become the Happiest

PRESIDENT IKEDA: It was in Okinawa some thirty-three years ago, on December 2, 1964, that I first took up my pen to write the novel *The Human Revolution*. Visiting the islands, I could not help crying out: "Nothing is more barbarous than war. Nothing is more cruel." My undying hope for the Okinawan people is that, as people who have experienced the cruelest pain and suffering, they should experience supreme happiness and joy. I can't begin to express how happy I am that our friends in Okinawa are living such long and healthy lives.

MATSUOKA: The "mother of kosen-rufu" in Okinawa, Tamae Nakama, the first women's leader there, is now seventy-one. She is a perfect example of someone who is making the most of the third stage of life.

PRESIDENT IKEDA: Yes. She has really worked hard for kosen-rufu in Okinawa. Faith means courage and taking action. She has said: "The struggle can't be won unless you keep taking action, unless you keep moving forward, going round to visit people until your legs ache, and become as hard as iron. You have to walk and walk and walk until you develop those iron legs." She is a wonderful example for us all.

Her husband had been born in Okinawa, but he was educated in Hawaii and then moved to Tokyo, where he met his wife. After they were married, Mr. Nakama decided to go back and settle in Okinawa, and the couple arrived there together by boat on New Year's Day, 1956. Mrs. Nakama was born and raised in Tokyo.

MATSUOKA: During your first visit to Okinawa in July 1960, the Okinawa Chapter was established and Mrs. Nakama was appointed as the first chapter women's leader. The day before the inaugural chapter meeting, you visited Mr. Nakama to pay your respects and confirm her appointment with him, and he told you that he would fully support his wife in her new responsibilities.

SASAKI: That night, Mr. Nakama said to his wife: "We're involved in a revolution, so I want you to devote your full energies to your Soka Gakkai activities. I promise not to complain if one of my shirts is missing a button or my shoes aren't polished. Give it all that you've got. Work hard together with President Ikeda. You promised him that you would."

PRESIDENT IKEDA: It was at the height of the July heat, but Mr. Nakama, with his strong eyebrows and handsome face, was wearing a necktie. When I said that I wanted to ask his wife to take on the position of Okinawa's women's leader, he replied, "My dear wife will be working for the people of Okinawa, and I will support her in any way I can." I met him the following year and the year after that, each time offering my thanks for his cooperation.

MATSUOKA: Before she started practicing Nichiren Buddhism, Mrs. Nakama was very sick and weak, and she used to spend about half of every month in bed. But after sensing that her mission lay in helping the people of Okinawa, she became this hardworking woman with legs of iron, and continued to make ceaseless efforts to promote our movement to this day.

SASAKI: Her husband died in 1970, leaving her a widow at only forty-three. His last words to her were, "Work for kosen-rufu with President Ikeda."

PRESIDENT IKEDA: Mr. Nakama was hospitalized in Tokyo, and I sent my greetings to him on several occasions. I told Mrs. Nakama that everything would be fine in Okinawa and she should spend her time taking care of her husband; but she couldn't bring herself to stay away from Okinawa too long. That is how devoted she was to her adopted home. Kosen-rufu is a revolution. Without the selfless devotion, without the ungrudging spirit of individuals such as this, that revolution cannot be accomplished.

SASAKI: Nevertheless, she loved and respected her husband and was deeply grateful to him. In the almost thirty years since his death, she has never failed to carry out his last instructions to her, working day and night for the cause of kosen-rufu. She cares nothing for her own comfort, only that of others. When she sees young members working late at the community center, for instance, she'll go and fix them a snack of some kind, like hot miso soup with fresh fish.

MATSUOKA: As I said earlier, she is a model for how one can be productive and fulfilled in the third stage of life. She has said, "I have decided that I will continue to work for kosen-rufu all my life. That is how I will end my days. As long as President Ikeda is still healthy and devoting himself tirelessly, I am determined to do so too. I want to repay President Ikeda for making Okinawa a land of peace."

"You Will Grow Younger"

PRESIDENT IKEDA: Nichiren writes, "Whatever trouble occurs, regard it as no more than a dream, and think only of the Lotus Sutra" (WND-1, 502). When all is said and done, those who dedicate their lives to kosen-rufu, just as the Daishonin instructs, will triumph. He also says, "You will grow younger" (WND-1, 464).

If you continue to advance on the path of kosen-rufu, life force will naturally well up from the depths of your being.

As the years pass, you will grow younger and younger and live to the end of your days filled with vitality. That is what Buddhism teaches us, and that is what so many of our worthy seniors and comrades in faith have shown us through the example of their lives.

SASAKI: More than forty years have passed since Mrs. Nakama left Tokyo to settle in Okinawa, so I felt it was worthwhile to ask her the Okinawan secret of long life. She said that she thought it was because Okinawans are essentially "good-natured people." They are broad-minded. The pace of their lives is relaxed. And they care about others, placing great value on human relationships. Those, she suggested, were the secrets to their long lives. She says that when she comes to Tokyo, the city is too fast-paced, and she doesn't feel comfortable anymore.

PRESIDENT IKEDA: I see. Being a "good-natured person" is the secret to long life. I suppose that is true. A person who cares for others is valued and treasured by others. I think that tradition is alive and well in Okinawa.

CHAPTER 10

A Noble Spirit of Mutual Aid and Support

SASAKI: Yoshihiko Ojiri, chief secretary of the Soka Gakkai's science and academic division in Okinawa Prefecture, has offered us some interesting information from the perspective of health science about the longevity of the inhabitants of Okinawa. He is an instructor at the Faculty of Medicine of the University of the Ryukyus in Okinawa, and he teaches a course in elementary public health. Toward the end of 1996, the university embarked on an extensive study into the relationship between longevity and Okinawa's climate and regional characteristics. Dr. Ojiri is one of the researchers involved in that project.

MATSUOKA: It is widely accepted that blockages of blood vessels in the brain are a major cause of senility, and that bone fractures arising from osteoporosis cause many elderly people to become bedridden. How, then, can we prevent blood vessel damage and the thinning of bone mass?

Dr. Ojiri has been studying what effect exercise patterns have on cholesterol levels and bone density and has been collating scientific data to demonstrate the importance of exercise. His next step is to make a statistical comparison between the Okinawa data collected and that from other prefectures.

PRESIDENT IKEDA: That's a most meaningful field of research. Wisdom is the secret to good health. Wisdom allows us to ensure our well-being. We need to be aware of how to prevent illness before it occurs and how to preserve our health so that we can go about our activities with zest and energy. We mustn't simply succumb passively to old age; instead, we should engage it head-on in a positive and active way. The field of health science offers us a special type of wisdom that teaches us how to accomplish that. Today, many universities around the world have made this field a separate department of specialization. Japan, however, lags behind these moves.

SASAKI: Dr. Ojiri offers two important factors in achieving long life: (1) dealing successfully with stress and (2) physical activity. He points out that since there is no way to avoid stress in life, it is important to deal with it successfully and learn to prevent it from accumulating.

Master Your Mind and Transform Despair Into Hope

PRESIDENT IKEDA: Recently [on September 20, 1997], I met with Martin Seligman, professor of psychology at the University of Pennsylvania and president-elect of the American Psychological Association. Dr. Seligman remarked that people who focus only on themselves and their own concerns tend to easily fall victim to pessimism.

The death of a loved one, divorce, business failure—these are among life's most stressful and trying events. The older one is, the more devastating they can be. You feel as if you are all alone in pitch darkness, suffering and in pain. There are feelings of isolation and sorrow—which is perfectly natural since we're only human.

Nevertheless, or rather precisely because of this, it's important that we look deep into our hearts and become painters, artists, and strive actively to repaint our minds in the colors of hope. As long as we remain preoccupied with our own troubles, as long as we allow ourselves to blindly follow the impulsive dictates of our mind, our sufferings will continue. What we must do is become the masters of our minds, not let them master us, and consciously redirect our thoughts in a positive and pleasant direction and help others around us do the same.

MATSUOKA: That is the secret to dealing with stress, isn't it? Dr. Ojiri has remarked that the Soka Gakkai embodies a system whereby members can discuss their problems with others, a sort of counseling system that has evolved quite naturally within Soka Gakkai activities. There are many leaders, and a member can talk to them about the problems he or she is encountering. If one leader's advice doesn't seem helpful, there's always another leader to turn to, and another, until the member is satisfied.

PRESIDENT IKEDA: Sometimes seeking advice from many leaders may not be necessary. President Toda encouraged each member to find a trusted senior in faith with whom they could feel free to discuss anything.

Essentially, our own mind or thinking holds the key to dealing successfully with problems that cause anxiety or stress. So in that respect here, too, "our heart is what matters most."

SASAKI: With regard to the second factor in long life, physical activity, I think we can learn a great deal by looking at the case of Ogimi, a village on Okinawa's main island that prides itself in the longevity of its residents. One section of Ogimi, known as Kijoka, produces the famous abaca (banana plant) cloth of Okinawa, and its residents are notably long lived.

The folk craft of weaving Okinawan abaca cloth, incidentally, has been designated as an Important Intangible Cultural Property of Japan.

MATSUOKA: As a member of the University of the Ryukyus research team, Dr. Ojiri conducted a detailed survey of the daily routines of the elderly residents of this area. Most of them, they found, continued to spin abaca thread well after age ninety. This physical activity kept their hands and bodies nimble and supple. At the same time, the elderly residents had a real sense of contributing to the community, because they were helping produce this famous local product. This seemed to be related to their longevity.

PRESIDENT IKEDA: Speaking of abaca cloth, two years ago when I was at the Okinawa Training Center, some elderly members—whom I believe were from Kijoka—showed me how the cloth was woven. It was so interesting that I went to see the demonstration twice.

MATSUOKA: Yes, you met Kazu Taira (eighty-six), Miki Nakada (eighty-two), and Yasu Maeda (eighty). After shaking your hand on that occasion, one of them remarked with emotion how they would never forget your gentle touch nor Mrs. Ikeda's kind smile as she wished them continued good health.

SASAKI: When we asked them the secret of their longevity, they offered all sorts of different reasons. One said it was Okinawa's great weather and fresh air; another declared it was eating plenty of vegetables; another chimed in that she ate a lot of pork, and she just loved it. One further suggested that it was just working all the time, trying to make ends meet.

Light a Lantern for Others, and Your Own Way Will Be Brightened as Well

PRESIDENT IKEDA: It is often pointed out that Okinawa retains the positive neighborly values of a horizontal, egalitarian society. For example, in Ogimi Village, passersby will turn on their neighbors' lights for them when it gets dark. No one wants to return home to a dark house, the thinking goes, so they kindly turn the lights on so that the occupants can return to a bright house. Most people in the village never lock their doors. There are no thefts or other criminal activities. It's a place where people can live in peace and security.

In Nichiren's writings, we find the passage, "If one lights a fire for others, one will brighten one's own way" (WND-2, 1060). In an aging society, the spirit of lighting a lantern for others is very important. In the end, it means brightening your own way as well.

MATSUOKA: In an environment such as Ogimi, the solitary death of an elderly person living alone, which happens in so many big cities, is unthinkable, isn't it?

SASAKI: People in Ogimi share the extra vegetables they grow—the tomatoes, cucumbers, and bitter melons that they pick—with their neighbors. When they have extra, they just leave them on their neighbors' doorsteps.

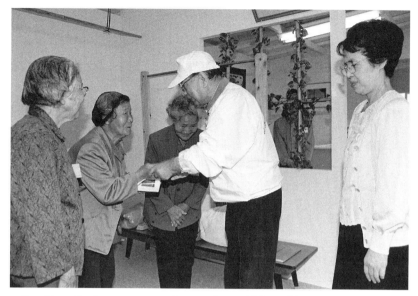

President Ikeda encourages the members of Many Treasure Group from Kijyoka, Ogimi Village, at the Okinawa Training Center, March 1995.

PRESIDENT IKEDA: Local cooperation and mutual assistance are carried out in an extremely natural way, without the formality or bureaucracy we see in other parts of Japan. I think that's wonderful. The Okinawan spirit of mutual aid, known as *yuimar,* is famous. Labor-intensive activities such as sugar-cane harvesting are carried out collectively, every family taking turns helping the others. This same spirit of sharing no doubt is what sustains Okinawans' longevity.

MATSUOKA: The production of abaca cloth is another example of sharing. There are some thirty steps in the process of making the cloth. First, the raw material for the cloth, abaca plants, which grow to some six feet high, have to be chopped down; then, they are boiled, washed, and hazed with bamboo pincers to comb out the fibers. Next, they are dried, separated into threads, and boiled again in a big pot. Then they are wrung out and dyed, and still the list goes on. There are an unbelievable number of steps to the process, many requiring considerable physical strength. Finely honed skill and craftsmanship are also needed to produce the cloth.

SASAKI: The women of the village divide up the work based on their levels of expertise, making it a joint production. That shared work is fun, they say, and also gives them a sense of purpose and fulfillment. They have a job that they can stay active at throughout their lives.

PRESIDENT IKEDA: I have heard that Kazu Taira is a member of the Abaca Cloth Preservation Society and an expert weaver. She made a strong impression on me. Her open and frank personality was revealed in the laughter lines that adorned her face; I'm sure that smile helped her sail through whatever troubles she may have encountered in her long life.

SASAKI: Kazu was raised by her widowed mother, who half-forced her to learn spinning as a craft by which she could support herself. She says she loathed spinning when she was young and went to work instead at a textile plant outside Okinawa just to get away from it. But now she says: "I am grateful to my mother for teaching me to work with my hands. Yes, now that I'm eighty, I am finally truly grateful to her."

Kazu and her two friends are known to cheerfully declare: "We're busy. We've got Soka Gakkai activities. We don't have time to waste." The local Soka Gakkai chapter women's leader remarked that the three women often declare they've had "an idle day" if they take even an hour or two out of their work day to attend to something else. The younger people can't keep up with them, she says with admiration.

PRESIDENT IKEDA: There is an expression that symbolizes the Okinawan spirit, *Nuchi du takara*, or "Life is a treasure." In Nichiren's writings we also find the passage, "Life is the most precious of all treasures" (WND-1, 955). Both reveal a profound philosophy of the innate sanctity of life.

The Okinawan dialect contains no words to express pity toward others in a patronizing or condescending way. Instead, Okinawans say *chimugurisa*, which means "my heart aches." This, of course, is the same as the Soka Gakkai spirit of sharing or feeling others' sufferings as our own.

Do you know the Okinawan expression *ichariba chode*?

SASAKI: It means "All whom we meet are our brothers," doesn't it?

PRESIDENT IKEDA: Yes. This is another expression of the wisdom of an egalitarian society. Buddhism teaches us that "You have come to owe a debt of gratitude to all living beings. And since this is so, you should help all of them to attain Buddhahood" (WND-2, 637). A place where people are valued, where human relations are treasured has all the vital ingredients for a society in which people live long and fulfilled lives.

In Okinawa, it's customary for relatives and neighbors to celebrate a person's longevity. One of the most interesting celebrations is that for reaching one's ninety-seventh year (one's ninety-sixth birthday). It's called *kajimaya,* which means "pinwheel." In this celebration, the birthday person rides through the streets of town in an open convertible. He or she holds a pinwheel, as do all the people who line the streets. The meaning of the celebration is said to be that in one's ninety-seventh year one becomes young at heart again, and playing with a pinwheel symbolizes that child-like innocence. Whatever the true origins of this celebration may be, the community's respect and celebration also become important motivations for people to live long.

SASAKI: Soka Gakkai Vice President Kunihiro Mitsumori of Okinawa has said that in the capital, Naha, and other urbanized areas of the prefecture, these wonderful old traditions are on the wane. As a result, many people have great hopes that the Soka Gakkai's network of friendship and sense of community—created through its regular local gatherings and monthly discussion meetings—will spread further throughout these areas, where they feel it will help preserve the Okinawan spirit.

PRESIDENT IKEDA: In the early years of our activities on Okinawa, the strong egalitarian ties that bound people in the community posed a great hurdle to our propagation activities. It was difficult for an individual to be the first in their family to join the Soka Gakkai. But as we continued to emphasize the organization's goals and to demonstrate solid actual proof of faith in everyday life, the circle of understanding steadily expanded throughout Okinawan society.

I think you could call it a case of reaching a tipping point. Once we had reached that point, understanding toward Nichiren Buddhism rapidly spread and deepened. That is also due to the Okinawan character, I think.

MATSUOKA: Mr. Mitsumori's mother is ninety-one, but still very hale and hearty. She was born on Taketomijima (one of the islands that comprise Okinawa Prefecture), and she was the first in her extended family of siblings, parents, and relatives to join the Soka Gakkai. Mr. Mitsumori related that his mother's decision upset her family in the beginning due to their lack of understanding about the practice, but when they saw the positive changes she underwent as a result of challenging her human revolution, they quickly joined the Soka Gakkai too—a reflection of just how strong the family ties were. Today, every member of that extended family practices Nichiren Buddhism.

Let Us Improve the Quality of Our Lives

PRESIDENT IKEDA: There is a difference between simply living a long life and living a rich and rewarding life. What's really important is how much we can improve the quality of our lives during our stay here on earth—however long it may be. For example, a life can be fulfilled and productive even if it is short by time's measure. Quality is the true value, not quantity.

I recently met with Ved Prakash Nanda, the associate provost of the University of Denver [September 1997]. Dr. Nanda is a world-renowned scholar of international law and a good friend. Though he is struggling with illness himself, he expressed concern for my health. "I am praying with all my heart that you will live to over one hundred," he told me. He also shared a famous Indian saying: "One must live one thousand years. Live one thousand years as if each year has ten thousand days."

The important thing is that we live each day without regret, moving forward in our work for kosen-rufu; that we continue to cherish in our hearts a shining purpose and reason for living, whatever our age. Leading each day in this way is the key to a life of profound satisfaction and fulfillment.

A Forty-Six-Year Partnership of Devoted Service to Kosen-rufu

MATSUOKA: In response to our request, Mrs. Ikeda has joined our dialogue.

Thank you both very much for making this possible.

PRESIDENT IKEDA: Don't thank me. It was entirely up to my wife. She finally decided that if she could be of any help, she'd be glad to participate.

SASAKI: Thank you again, Mrs. Ikeda.

MRS. IKEDA: I really don't know if I have anything useful to contribute, but I'll do my best.

Serving the Members

MATSUOKA: *(Addressing Mr. and Mrs. Ikeda)* You were married on May 3, 1952, and this year [1998] you will celebrate your forty-sixth wedding anniversary. I would like to express my most deep-felt gratitude for the utterly selfless dedication and commitment with which you have worked together for the progress of kosen-rufu, the development of the Soka Gakkai, and the happiness and welfare of the members over those long years.

SASAKI: In a poem that you dedicated to the members in Tokyo's Ota Ward, where you were born and raised, President Ikeda, you related the story of how Mrs. Ikeda, when she was still a young girl with pigtails, went to meet Tsunesaburo Makiguchi, the Soka Gakkai's founder, at Ota's Yaguchinowatashi Station and guide him to a discussion meeting being held at her home. That anecdote points up the long history of Mrs. Ikeda's faith.

MRS. IKEDA: Yes, I was an elementary school student at the time. I went with my mother to meet Mr. Makiguchi at the station. He patted me on the head and said: "How nice of you to come to meet me! Thank you!"

In those days, there were only a few little shops in front of the station. There were so few houses that you could see the banks of the nearby Tamagawa River from the station.

As we walked toward our home, I remember thinking that Mr. Makiguchi was very old. But the moment he took his place at the discussion meeting, he was transformed. He sat up straight and spoke in ringing tones. He had tremendous authority and dignity.

PRESIDENT IKEDA: That's the mark of a true leader. When the time comes to exercise leadership, a leader acts with confidence and strength. The more responsibility a leader bears, the more youthful and energetic he or she becomes.

It's important to note that right up to the time Mr. Makiguchi was arrested for alleged violation of the notorious Peace Preservation Law [used by the militarists to crackdown on any opposition], he was active everywhere, even in places like Yaguchinowatashi, on the fringes of Ota Ward. To the very last, he was out among the people, indefatigable in his efforts to travel to meet and talk with others about Nichiren Buddhism. This is the spirit from which the Soka Gakkai springs, and it offers us a model for all eternity.

MRS. IKEDA: Sometime after the discussion meeting began, three members of the Special Higher Police arrived and stood in the hallway facing the garden to observe the meeting. Suddenly, in the middle of Mr. Makiguchi's words, they shouted: "Stop right there! That's enough!" Looking back on it, I recall that they interrupted just after Mr. Makiguchi had denounced the policy of forcing all Japanese to accept the Shinto talisman as part of the militarist government's drive for "thought unification" to strengthen the war effort.

As a child, I remember being frightened at that moment, but when I asked my mother later she said that she wasn't the least bit afraid because Mr. Makiguchi was so dignified and unwavering in his convictions.

By the time the discussion meeting came to an end, the three members of the Special Higher Police had disappeared.

PRESIDENT IKEDA: The struggles of Mr. Makiguchi and Mr. Toda in prison are what made today's Soka Gakkai and the miraculous progress we have seen in the kosen-rufu movement possible. Giving one's life for one's beliefs is the greatest honor for a person of faith. I, too, have devoted myself completely, exerting myself unceasingly without any thought to my own well-being, for the sake of our movement. I want to bestow the highest praises on those members who have fought valiantly alongside me.

Mr. Toda's Words: "I'm Counting on You"

MRS. IKEDA: We have never really been able to enjoy a private life or the pleasures of ordinary domesticity. When we were married, Mr. Toda looked at me solemnly and said with deep earnestness: "I'm counting on you to support Daisaku. The future of the Soka Gakkai depends upon it." Since that day I have done everything I could to help and support my husband.

PRESIDENT IKEDA: I remember once at a New Year's celebration, Mr. Toda wept openly, tears streaming down his face. "Your life is bound to be short," he said. "What will become of the Soka Gakkai?" On another occasion, he said he would gladly give me the remaining days of his life so that I might live on to carry out my mission. Those words also represented a strict injunction and impassioned plea on the part of my mentor, who knew that his own life was ebbing away, that I improve my health and get well and strong.

Since that time I have always tried to pay attention to my health, but in the endeavor to establish a firm foundation for kosen-rufu I have found myself working and traveling day and night around the clock, without much time to think of my own needs. I am deeply grateful to my wife, whose unfailing support has made my work possible.

Mr. and Mrs. Ikeda around the time of their marriage, 1952.

MRS. IKEDA: Having heard Mr. Toda say that my husband wouldn't live very long, my mother was beside herself with worry when he became Soka Gakkai president. She fretted over what would become of us, his wife and children, if he should die young.

I responded to this by doing everything I could think of to help him stay well and healthy. Our room was very small, so sometimes when he was really exhausted, I insisted on putting my futon in the hallway and sleeping there, so as not to disturb him when I got up early in the morning.

MATSUOKA: I have heard that on one occasion, when you saw President Ikeda hard at work despite his deep fatigue, you prayed that all his sickness might be visited upon you in his place.

MRS. IKEDA: It was a difficult time for the Soka Gakkai. I was healthy, and I wanted to do anything I could to lessen my husband's sufferings. That was my prayer.

PRESIDENT IKEDA: Yes, and after that, she came down with something and had to take to her bed! I wrote her a letter from my travels, chiding her gently that she had only made me worry more and that she shouldn't be so foolish to pray for ill health again.

MRS. IKEDA: I had never been sick until then. When I became ill myself, I realized I had never really appreciated how bad he must feel all the time, suffering as he did in those days from extremely poor health and a nagging fever. It was a good lesson for me. From then on, I have always prayed that we're *both* healthy.

One thing that I have learned over the years is that there is nothing more wonderful than being able to sit before the Gohonzon as husband and wife and pray together.

Mr. Makiguchi's Legacy

SASAKI: When I attended a discussion meeting of the Takanawa Chapter (Minato Ward, Tokyo), a former pupil of Mr. Makiguchi's had just joined the Soka Gakkai, an event that was celebrated with great enthusiasm at the meeting. The name of the new member is Kiyo Sudo and she is now seventy-eight years old! She enrolled in Shirokane Elementary School—where Mr. Makiguchi was principal—in April 1927. She recalls from those days that Mr. Makiguchi was a very dignified man with a commanding presence, yet also very warm and gentle. She remembered him once having attended a school field trip with the students to Hibiya Park. This was in 1929, a time when Mr. Makiguchi was certainly still grieving over the loss of his own children, who had died one after another.

MATSUOKA: Mrs. Sudo joined the Soka Gakkai when she learned from her hairdresser, a women's division member, that Mr. Makiguchi was the organization's founder.

Mrs. Sudo had always loved and respected Mr. Makiguchi, so she decided to become a member without a moment's hesitation.

MRS. IKEDA: That is amazing. After all these years, Mr. Makiguchi continues to bring in new members!

MATSUOKA: Mrs. Sudo relates that Mr. Makiguchi always walked from Meguro Station to the school, and when he encountered students on his way he would lift his hat and greet them pleasantly. At lunchtime there were always a stack of lunchboxes wrapped in white handkerchiefs left in the school office for students who, for family reasons, couldn't bring their own lunch. These had been provided by Mr. Makiguchi out of his own pocket, she said.

PRESIDENT IKEDA: That's just like Mr. Makiguchi. He believed that education's foremost goal is the happiness and welfare of children.

Mr. Makiguchi paid close attention to his own health as well it seems. I often walked to Mr. Toda's house, on call as I was at all hours of the day and night. It was not far from Shirokane Elementary School, and it's a brisk fifteen-minute walk. That was Mr. Makiguchi's walk too.

Live a Life That Will Be Remembered Forever!

SASAKI: Mrs. Sudo showed me an old photograph she has of herself and her classmates with Mr. Makiguchi when they were in the second grade. There are now four of the class who are Soka Gakkai members. One of them, her best friend in those school days, Sadako, later married Mr. Makiguchi's third son, Yozo. Sadako was overjoyed when she learned that her old school friend had recently joined the Soka Gakkai.

MATSUOKA: The other two classmates who are Soka Gakkai members are Sumiko Miki and Mitsuko Asao. Mr. Makiguchi resigned as principal of Shirokane Elementary School when Mrs. Asao (a resident of Tokyo's Shinagawa Ward) was a third grader, but she still remembers him vividly. Mrs. Miki is a vice women's leader of Tokyo's Koto Ward. The way in which you have continued to honor Mr. Makiguchi, she says, is a tremendously moving model of the solemn path of mentor and disciple.

PRESIDENT IKEDA: The way we live determines the way we are spoken about and remembered in the future. That is, in a sense, how we live on in this world after our passing.

Having turned seventy, I have resolved to work even harder than I have heretofore. Looking back, when I was young I worked with single-minded intensity but sometimes

I wasted energy because of overzealousness. After reaching sixty, however, all my efforts are productive and fruitful; there is no wasted energy. I believe that I work as hard and effectively now in one year as I did in five in my youth.

Giving earnest thought to the future is the world of humanity; living only for the moment is the world of animality. My foremost concern right now is leaving the future of our movement in capable hands—fostering and educating the youth is the only way to ensure this. What kind of example can I leave for them as Mr. Toda's disciple? All I can do is dedicate myself to kosen-rufu to the last moment of my life.

CHAPTER 12

A Shared Journey for Worldwide Kosen-rufu

MATSUOKA: With the increased number of President Ikeda's trips overseas, I'm sure that the demands placed upon you have also grown, Mrs. Ikeda. We'd be happy if you could share with us what some of those travels were like.

MRS. IKEDA: Certainly. As you know, in many countries overseas, it is customary for a husband and wife to participate in social occasions as a couple. When our children were small, of course, I couldn't travel, but now I usually go along.

PRESIDENT IKEDA: She often jokes that she's the "garnish" accompanying the main dish, but she's always a great help. When I meet with various dignitaries, they almost always have their spouses with them. Over the years, in addition to attending SGI events and encouraging members, my meetings and dialogues with nonmembers have also increased significantly. That is why my wife started accompanying me.

A Smile That Warms and Soothes

MRS. IKEDA: In the early years, we had very few headquarters staff traveling with us, and I took care of everything myself. We'd arrive at our hotel, and the first thing I'd do was unpack. My next task was to get him to rest. Once I'd made sure he was relaxing, I'd cook some rice and prepare some simple food in the bathroom. That was my role, and it suited me perfectly.

SASAKI: As a reporter for the *Seikyo Shimbun,* I have accompanied you and President Ikeda on overseas trips, and you contribute such a warmth and ease to the atmosphere.

I found that especially true when President Ikeda first began visiting what was then the Soviet Union [in 1974]. The Soviet Union was, after all, a highly ideological nation, and while its leaders did show an appreciation of the Soka Gakkai's movement for culture, peace, and education, there were many pointed discussions on the subjects of religion and history.

Your warm smile was an important factor in those meetings and allowed both sides to advance to a deeper mutual understanding, I thought.

MRS. IKEDA: As you know, wherever my husband goes, he's always breaking new ground, always pioneering. He's quite determined. As a result, I think, he often comes on rather strong. I am happy if my presence does anything to make things go more smoothly and contribute to mutual understanding.

PRESIDENT IKEDA: The crucial issue for me has always been whether my health will hold out for the length of the visit. My wife's help on that score is invaluable. I also know that after I'm asleep she often stays up late into the night chanting for me on the sofa in another room.

MRS. IKEDA: I don't know whether I should say this or not, but my husband is always running at full speed. His mind is always working, he's always giving attention to a hundred things at once. The only time his brain gets any rest is when he's asleep. That's why I make him go to sleep. The moment his eyes are open, he's running here and there again. Isn't that right?

PRESIDENT IKEDA: It's just my nature, the way I am. You can change many things, they say, but not your nature.

Mr. Toda was really a wonderful mentor. Everything I am is the result of the training I received from him. He was incredibly sharp—always quick to discern others' thoughts and feelings. If he sensed I was holding something back, he would tell me to come out with it; otherwise I'd be making an enemy of my mentor. He really kept me on my toes, at all times. I was just a raw youth when we met, but he trained, forged, and polished me.

Mr. Toda stressed the importance of caring for the

members' welfare, personally making oneself familiar with their needs and desires and giving them hope and courage. He pounded the secret of leadership into me—in other words, that working for the members is the key to the development of the Soka Gakkai.

MRS. IKEDA: In his youth, they used to call my husband the X-ray. I'm sure it was because of his deep concern for people, but they used to say he knew what you were thinking, that he could see through you at a glance. That was how wholeheartedly he gave of himself for kosen-rufu. Seeing this, I was determined to do everything in my power to assist him, so that he could dedicate himself to the work that I knew he alone could do. We often say that he's the speedy hare and I'm the slow and steady tortoise. . . . No, let's make that the crane and the tortoise, so that we'll both live a long time![34]

MATSUOKA: I hope you don't mind me asking such a personal question, but has President Ikeda ever taken you to task over something?

MRS. IKEDA: Yes, when I deserved it. I'm not perfect, after all. Of course, he has never reproved me without justification. He always had a very good reason. One of the times I remember best was when he asked me to send a photograph to a member.

He had paid a visit to the terminally ill brother of a

member and took a photograph of him while he was there. When it was developed, he asked me to send it to the member. But I delayed . . . not as long as a week, but perhaps four or five days. I thought that I should send a letter or note with it, and I was waiting until I had the time to write one.

I finally sent it, late, and it arrived just two or three hours after the member's brother died. That's when he scolded me. I had no excuse. I felt so sorry for what I had done. If only I had sent the photograph when he had asked. You cannot imagine the shock and remorse I felt. It was a good lesson. Yes, I still remember that.

SASAKI: Assisting President Ikeda is a very demanding task. I'm sure you're under constant stress.

MATSUOKA: Incidentally, I understand that you also meet with prefectural women's leaders when they gather in Tokyo for the monthly prefectural leaders meetings and that they share with you news about their activities in each region.

MRS. IKEDA: Recently I've been so busy that I can't always do so regularly. And when I do, it's not as if I'm offering guidance or acting in a leadership role. Women—myself included—want to have someone to listen to their thoughts and ideas. They also have many things that they want to communicate to President Ikeda. I always have the spirit that if listening to what they have to say imparts some joy and encouragement and helps them engage in their activities with renewed energy, I'm only too glad to do it. After all, they're all working so hard.

Respect Our Precious Members "As If They Were Buddhas"

PRESIDENT IKEDA: I think it's very important to listen to what women have to say. And men shouldn't berate women. They don't have the right. They should have nothing but praise for women's efforts. Nichiren Daishonin said that we show people of strong faith and who have made vigorous efforts to propagate the Mystic Law "the kind of respect one would show to a Buddha" (OTT, 193).

I never forget for even a fraction of a moment that it has been the hard work of the members of our women's division that has made the Soka Gakkai what it is today. Women bear an enormous burden. Many have to take care of their families, husbands, children, and parents, facing the innumerable challenges of daily life as well as the larger issues of life that we all confront. That's no doubt why they know, from direct experience, how important faith is. Men in our organization who do not value the contribution of our women's division members do not deserve to be leaders.

MRS. IKEDA: I'm very grateful that my husband has always supported my growth.

Going back to our overseas travels, I especially recall 1974. We were very busy that year with many overseas trips.

SASAKI: Yes, in January of that year you went to Hong Kong, then North, Central, and South America in March and April. In the fall, you traveled to the Soviet Union. Your first trip to the People's Republic of China took place in May, and you went there again in December. You hardly had time to catch your breath; it was such a travel-filled year.

MATSUOKA: Brazil was also on the agenda that year, wasn't it?

PRESIDENT IKEDA: We applied for visas while we were in the United States, and we waited at the Malibu Training Center[35] outside Los Angeles for them to come through. While we were waiting, we spent our days meeting with local members. At the time, unfounded, negative rumors about the SGI were circulating in Brazil, and there was strong opposition to us entering the country. In the end, we couldn't get visas and had to change our plans.

SASAKI: The night that it was decided you wouldn't go to Brazil, you called the then SGI-Brazil general director from the phone on the second floor of the Malibu Training Center. I remember you saying, in a forceful, determined voice: "I don't want you showing any disappointment. Please present a cheerful face to the members and encourage them with all your might! Give them my fondest regards too! I'll definitely make it there one day!"

Afterward you said: "I may not be able to go to Brazil, but there's still the rest of the world. The universe awaits us!" The breadth of your scope, the depth of your vision, took my breath away. It was a quiet night; you could hear the waves lapping on the beach of the Malibu Coast.

PRESIDENT IKEDA: That's when things really started to happen, wasn't it? The leaders and members of SGI-Brazil prayed earnestly and opened the way for kosen-rufu in their country. Their prayers were answered and they made a firm foundation for tremendous future growth, all through the power of their strong prayers.

Everything is always changing; the only indestructible, unchanging thing is Nam-myoho-renge-kyo. If you earnestly chant, you are guaranteed to open new opportunities. You will achieve an unsurpassable state of being. Today, SGI-Brazil is making the best efforts in the world.

MATSUOKA: Eighteen years later, you finally visited Brazil. A wonderful culture festival was held, and we were all impressed by the vibrant energy of the Brazilian members, who were making remarkable contributions to their local communities and society at large. After that visit, parks and streets were named after you and Mr. Makiguchi and Mr. Toda, and a number of schools incorporated the principles of Mr. Makiguchi's value-creating education into their curricula. Today Brazil understands the SGI and has great hopes for the role it will play in Brazilian society.

PRESIDENT IKEDA: Those who worked so hard together to achieve this deserve the highest praise. This only goes to show that those who fight with all their might to triumph over painful obstacles and setbacks win without fail in the end and contribute to the advance of kosen-rufu.

MRS. IKEDA: Nineteen seventy-four was a hard year, what with the very busy schedule and the uncertainty of our itinerary during our travels. But I know that the struggles of the members in each country far surpassed anything we experienced.

My husband presented me with a poem during that trip.

SASAKI: Could you share it with us?

MRS. IKEDA: Yes. "Opening the path / As I walk with you / My irreplaceable support." When we were young, he wrote me many letters. But when I received this poem, I was deeply moved that he saw our shared struggles side by side all these years as a joint effort to promote kosen-rufu. Whenever one of his dialogues is published, he says to me, "You're the one who made this book possible." And one year on my birthday (February 27), he handwrote a calligraphy for me that read: "I pay tribute to a golden history of global achievement for kosen-rufu."

CHAPTER 13

The Glory of an SGI Family

MATSUOKA: *(Addressing Mrs. Ikeda)* Actually, you are a great friend of the editing staff of the *Seikyo Shimbun*. On very important occasions when President Ikeda is meeting with visiting dignitaries, you often take notes in the place of reporters, and we are frequently indebted to you when it comes to writing our articles.

MRS. IKEDA: Thank you. My role is simply to help and support my husband. Our relationship is like the sun and the moon. I am merely the moon that shines in the sun's light.

PRESIDENT IKEDA: We both have different roles. There are times when the burning intensity and power of the sun are called for, and times when the soothing luminescence and serene wisdom of the moon is what's needed. A complementary relationship in which the partners cooperate and work together is a beautiful thing.

I remember Premier Zhou Enlai of China and his wife,

Madam Deng Yingchao. Even after the premier's death, Madame Deng carried on their joint struggle, working to serve the people as a fellow comrade. Sharing the same goals is so important.

MRS. IKEDA: Madame Deng always warmly embraced me as a daughter. I think she provided a wonderful, noble example, the way she kept alive the memory of her husband, with whom she had worked so hard for so long, and continued to devote herself to their shared ideals.

When Premier Zhou died, mourners sent many, many floral tributes of course. Among them was a small wreath with the note, "To my comrade-in-arms Enlai—from Little Chao." "Little Chao" was Madame Deng's nickname. I couldn't help feel that her overflowing emotions were distilled in that term *comrade in arms*. Incidentally, since we were just talking about the moon, I fondly recall a poem I received from President Toda:

May you possess both
The gentleness of the moonlight
And the strength of the Mystic Law.

Rather than needlessly competing with each other, I think it's important that both men and women devote their energies to working for the sake of others and for Buddhism while complementing each other. At the same time, I feel it's only natural that different people will play different roles in their efforts to realize this shared commitment.

MATSUOKA: Speaking of the moon, the first series of photographs you took, President Ikeda, were of the moon. As I recall, that was some twenty-eight years ago.

I vividly remember how sometimes you would set up your tripod and use many different lenses, from wide angle to zoom, to take photographs. Now you take photographs in a much freer fashion, don't you?

SASAKI: That reminds me of an incident in Moscow, more than twenty years ago. We were boating on the Moscow River at the invitation of Soviet Minister of Higher and Secondary Specialized Education V. P. Elyutin and discussing the subject of education.

At times you went to the very front of the boat, where you took several photographs of the beautiful spring greenery. You said that you would never see this scene again, and that you wanted to record it forever in your heart. This is photographing with the heart, you said.

PRESIDENT IKEDA: Yes, you take photographs with the heart. I think that if your sensibilities are rich and refined, you can capture the richness of nature's beauty. People's hearts are fickle, but nature never rejects us. Nature is all-accepting and all-embracing.

Determined Not to Waste a Moment

MATSUOKA: When you take photographs now, you just click the shutter without even looking through the viewfinder. A well-known photographer has described your work as the art of "capturing the moment with the eye of the heart." Jun Miki, long the president of the Japan Professional Photographer's Society and a great admirer of your photography over the years, once told me that many photographers lose the best moment to click the shutter because they spend too much time looking through the viewfinder. He said that you, on the other hand, always seem to capture the moment just perfectly, which is one of the reasons your photographs are so good. It's very difficult, he commented, to take photographs that reveal the depth and breadth of vision that yours do.

He also said: "President Ikeda's photographs are without affectation. I think the best way to describe them is 'artlessly beautiful' and 'effortlessly natural.' When you view them, you are struck by the infinite expanse of the photographer's spirit."

MRS. IKEDA: I think it's also important to remember that my husband isn't traveling around the world just to take photographs. He only manages to take photographs in the midst of an extremely demanding schedule.

PRESIDENT IKEDA: I just can't bear to waste a single moment. And sometimes my photographs serve to encourage and inspire our members. If the traveling exhibition of my photographs, "Dialogue With Nature," can provide an opportunity for members and I to share a broad and expansive vision of the world around us, nothing makes me happier.

MRS. IKEDA: We mustn't ever lose our sensitivity to beauty, our ability to appreciate fragrant flowers, beautiful music, or lovely paintings.

"Never Give In to Defeat"

SASAKI: May I ask, by the way, what your motto is, Mrs. Ikeda?

MRS. IKEDA: It's basically: "You may not always win, but never give in to defeat. Live in such a way that you are not defeated, no matter what the circumstances or situation."

PRESIDENT IKEDA: That's a crucial point. I am always emphasizing to the students of our Soka schools the importance of not letting themselves be defeated. As long as you're not defeated, you can always look forward to another opportunity for success in the future. The key is not getting down on yourself. You have to remember to value and treasure yourself.

MATSUOKA: When you were raising your children, Mrs. Ikeda, what did you always try to keep in mind as a mother?

MRS. IKEDA: How my own stress and tension, due to the many demands on my time, might adversely affect my children. We live in a world of relentless competition—not only in the adult world but even in the realm of children. That's the kind of age we live in. As a mother, I tried to keep some inner latitude in reserve so that I could create an atmosphere of emotional warmth and security for my children.

I think that the maternal instinct is the human emotion closest to nature. Nature is extraordinarily accepting, and I think mothers must be the same. If a mother is concerned only with her ambitions for her children—for example, that they get into a good school or earn good grades—her relationship with them will be cold and unfeeling. I think we should have a warmer, more relaxed attitude. Even if our children don't get top grades, for example, we should be happy and grateful that they are strong and healthy.

Teaching Children About Faith

SASAKI: If I may ask, how did you teach your children about faith?

MRS. IKEDA: I believe it's the same as in any other family. Gongyo is the basic practice in a Soka Gakkai family, and I started by teaching them to do it by reading it together, one word at a time. I discussed how we should instruct the children with my husband, and we both agreed that we should be neither too strict nor too lax. And he said, "It all comes down to the mother's faith in the end."

Morning gongyo is the way we start our day, so of course it's very important, but there were times when the children were running late for school. On those days, instead of making a fuss as they went out the door—which would probably have the reverse effect I hoped for—I would see them off with a smile and say reassuringly: "Don't worry. Today I'll do gongyo for you too."

PRESIDENT IKEDA: You have to use your head when teaching children about faith. But I have seen many, many families over the years and I think I can say that the faith of the children really does depend on the faith of their mother. Not that I'm letting fathers off the hook!

MRS. IKEDA: Our eldest son Hiromasa was born on April 28, 1953, the anniversary of the day on which Nichiren Daishonin publicly declared the teaching of Nam-myoho-renge-kyo (in 1253). My husband was away from Tokyo, attending a youth division meeting with President Toda.

Mr. Toda was overjoyed when he heard the news of our son's birth. Using a calligraphy brush, he wrote a poem on the folding fan he was using, "On the birth of your child /

how I rejoice / under the spring moon." That fan is one of our family treasures.

I often took Hiromasa along with me to Soka Gakkai activities from the time he was little. He even came along with me to many of the general meetings, leaders meetings, and lectures on Nichiren's writings led by President Toda. When my husband became president, Hiromasa was a first grader. From that time on, he always attended the annual headquarters leaders meeting as a member of the Ikeda family. Through that early involvement, he grew into a person who really loved the Soka Gakkai. He made his own file of clippings from the *Seikyo Shimbun* when he was a boy.

MATSUOKA: You and President Ikeda had three children— all boys.

MRS. IKEDA: Yes. Two years after Hiromasa, our second son, Shirohisa, was born. By that time, my husband was incredibly busy with Soka Gakkai work. Our third son, Takahiro, was born on April 11, 1958, just nine days after the death of President Toda on April 2. I was not able to participate in the ceremony of passing on the mission of kosen-rufu held on March 16 because I was so close to giving birth to Takahiro. But Mr. Toda asked me to come and visit him at the head temple where he was staying throughout that month, and I went there on March 18. I could see that his condition was very serious. That was our last meeting.

The period after Mr. Toda's death was a very difficult one for the organization. Many people predicted that the Soka Gakkai would disintegrate and disappear, so my husband was rushing all over Japan to encourage the members and was hardly ever home. The boys used to wait for him to return from his trips, looking forward eagerly to the little gifts they'd made him promise to bring back for them. He'd dash out the door saying: "Don't worry! I won't forget!" but I knew that he'd be so busy it would be impossible for him to find time to look for presents.

What I'd do is buy little gifts myself that the boys would probably like and put them away so that he could give them to the children when he returned from his trip.

MATSUOKA: I can just see the heartwarming scene you are describing.

How was President Ikeda's health in those days?

MRS. IKEDA: He tired very easily and in general was not in good health. He often woke up at night and wanted something cold to drink. I'm sure he had a fever. Even during winter, he always had night sweats, and when he woke in the morning his face was flushed.

I've always felt that my mission in life has been protecting my husband's health, so I am just overjoyed to see how unbelievably healthy he is now compared to his condition then.

SASAKI: I'm sure every member of the Soka Gakkai feels the same way.

MRS. IKEDA: I thank them all for their good wishes.

As our three sons grew older, each gradually gained his own appreciation of faith and began to apply himself to the practice and Soka Gakkai activities. I remember once, when our youngest son, Takahiro, was a high school student, he wanted to go on an astronomy field trip to Ogasawara (an island located more than five hundred miles south of Tokyo). I told him that he really should be attending a meeting of the future division that was taking place at the same time, but he said he had promised his classmates well in advance and he couldn't back out now.

I discussed the matter with his father, who said: "Our faith is something that we are involved in for our entire lives. Let's take the long view and allow him to go to Ogasawara. The important thing is that he sticks to his faith for the long haul." I confess that I, too, was relieved to hear him say those words.

As they matured into adulthood and their understanding of faith deepened, our children began, on their own initiative, to approach their father about Soka Gakkai activities and efforts for kosen-rufu not as a parent but as a mentor.

MATSUOKA: Even to us outsiders it's apparent that the relationship between President Ikeda and his sons is based on a spirit of mentor and disciple. It's very inspiring.

MRS. IKEDA: Our second son, Shirohisa, died at the age of twenty-nine, and like any parent, I was deeply grieved. I experienced the greatest sorrow and suffering that a person can know. Until you go through something like that yourself, you can't really relate to other people's pain and suffering. Everything in life is a lesson; such experiences, painful as they may be, make us what we are.

SASAKI: When I met Shirohisa's son and your grandson, Takahisa, the other day, I was surprised at how he'd grown. He's really quite a young gentleman, already a university student. I remember seeing you once, Mrs. Ikeda, talking happily with Takahisa and his mother. It was a wonderful sight. You looked so happy as you walked along holding hands with your grandson. I'll never forget it.

MRS. IKEDA: When Hiromasa graduated from Keio University and was looking for a job, he received offers from many companies. But perhaps because, as he was growing up, he had seen how dedicated his father was to education, he decided to become a teacher and went to work at Kansai Soka Junior and Senior High Schools.

Over the years, however, as my husband's exchanges with individuals and organizations outside the SGI have grown, Hiromasa has increasingly helped out by acting as his father's representative. I sincerely pray that he may always serve the members to his utmost.

Takahiro graduated from Soka University and also

decided to become a teacher. He took a post at Kansai Soka Elementary School. But lately we've been so busy that he's often acting as an assistant to his father as well.

MATSUOKA: I heard from President Ikeda that when Takahiro was thinking about what to do when he left school, you advised him, Mrs. Ikeda, to become an elementary school teacher rather than a university teacher, especially given the importance of elementary school teachers in terms of shaping their young students' lives.

MRS. IKEDA: Yes, I did say that. Both Mr. Makiguchi and Mr. Toda were elementary school teachers, after all. The Soka Gakkai (Value Creation Society) has its proud beginnings in the Soka Kyoiku Gakkai (Value-Creating Education Society).

PRESIDENT IKEDA: I make a clear distinction between my public and private lives, and so I haven't talked much about my family in the past, but our discussion in this installment has revealed all our secrets!

MATSUOKA: Thank you so much. Our readers made so many requests. . . .

PRESIDENT IKEDA: As Mr. Toda's disciple, I will devote myself to kosen-rufu as long as I live. My entire family is at the service of the Soka Gakkai, of our members. When I accepted the post of SGI president in Guam in 1975, I said to representatives from around the world: "I hope you do not seek after your own praise or glory but instead dedicate your whole lives to sowing the seeds of the Mystic Law for the sake of the peace of the whole world. I shall do the same thing." And that resolve will remain the same until the last day of my life.

CHAPTER 14

Faith Is the Key to Life's Triumph

MRS. IKEDA: When we recently visited the Philippines (February 1998), the sunsets over Manila Bay were as spectacular as their reputation. As I watched the solemn majesty of nature in all its glory, I thought to myself that our third stage of life should be just as magnificent and beautiful.

PRESIDENT IKEDA: Mr. Toda used to say that one's last years should be like a golden sunset. I absolutely agree, don't you? They are the words of a master of life. As the sun sinks below the horizon, it colors the world scarlet, announcing the end of one day and promising the brilliant arrival of the next.

MATSUOKA: During your visit to the Philippines, you met King Juan Carlos I of Spain. You conveyed your congratulations to him on his receiving the title of Knight Grand Cross of Rizal.[36]

SASAKI: King Juan Carlos is respected in Spain and throughout the world for facilitating his country's transition from a fascist dictatorship to democratic rule.

PRESIDENT IKEDA: Because of a military coup, his family had fled to exile in Portugal, and when he was ten years old he was sent back to Spain as a virtual hostage to the military regime. He underwent many hardships, but his father had taught him well. His father told him that a royal family must love their country and instructed him to travel about Spain so that the people would come to know him. He urged his son to stay in touch with people so that they could learn to know and understand one another, and finally to love one another.

That's just what he did. The young prince traveled throughout the country, from village to village. His situation was very uncertain. At any moment, he might be presented with the jeweled crown of his ancestors or an arrest warrant from the security forces. Walking a fine line between glory and destruction, he carefully listened and watched. He spent twenty years quietly biding his time. Soon after becoming king, he moved his country toward democracy. He withstood a coup d'état in 1981, winning at the same time the strong support of his people. All of this is very well known around the world.

MRS. IKEDA: It was the suffering he experienced as a youth that made him the great leader he is today. What ultimately decides our course in life, after all, are the struggles and hardships we've undergone and surmounted. Many years of experience have taught me that.

Like the Hiyoku *Bird, Like Intertwined Branches*

PRESIDENT IKEDA: Yes, that's so true.

My wife and I are like a bow and arrow, like the *hiyoku* bird,[37] like intertwined branches. We are companions and comrades in arms, who have fought almost half a century together in a fierce struggle, so fierce at times that we were uncertain whether we would live or die.

SASAKI: We introduced this at the very beginning of this series, but when you were interviewed by the editor of a women's magazine, President Ikeda, she asked you what kind of an award you would present to Mrs. Ikeda. You said how grateful you were for your wife's smile, and that you would give her the "Smile Award." You added, "When we are reborn, in the next life and the one after that, for all eternity, please be there for me." What was your reaction to that, Mrs. Ikeda?

MRS. IKEDA: My, my, I don't know what to say. Meeting my husband has been my greatest good fortune, the decisive event in my life. In Buddhist terms, I think you could say that it's due to fortune accumulated in my life from past existences. But I must continue to accumulate good fortune in this lifetime, or I will simply fall back like a stone rolling down a hill. I therefore make a conscious, active effort to do what I can each day to build the causes for future good fortune.

MATSUOKA: Just the other day we were speaking with your mother, Mrs. Ikeda. Though she's more than ninety, she's still full of energy. She told us about the morning that President Ikeda was inaugurated as the third Soka Gakkai president [on May 3, 1960].

MRS. IKEDA: At that time, we were living in a small house in Kobayashi-cho in Ota Ward [in Tokyo], and on that day my mother came to help me get my husband ready for his inauguration. My mother was attending the headquarters general meeting, too, but she first went to Kamata Station and found a taxi that would come and take my husband to the meeting. Then she got ready herself and rushed to the meeting by train.

PRESIDENT IKEDA: Yes. On that day, I remember taking a taxi to the Nihon University Auditorium in the Ryogoku area of Tokyo, where the inauguration was held. I rarely took taxis in those days. Even after becoming president, I'd commute to the Soka Gakkai Headquarters in Shinanomachi by train each day. I'd ride my bicycle to Kamata Station and take the Keihin Tohoku Line to Tokyo Station. There I transferred to the Chuo Line, then got off at Yotsuya and transferred again to the Sobu Line, which stopped at Shinanomachi. Ah, I was young in those days!

And the Soka Gakkai didn't own any cars then, either. We had very few facilities for our members; in fact, we had almost nothing.

SASAKI: At that time, I had just come to Tokyo from Yamagata Prefecture, and I was attending a private cram school in Ichigaya. When I transferred to the Sobu Line at Yotsuya Station one day, I saw you, standing on the platform reading a book and waiting for your train. I introduced myself and told you I was studying for university entrance exams, and you encouraged me. "Do your best!" you said.

Mr. and Mrs. Ikeda greet members as the train leaves the station, Bologna Station, Italy, 1994.

PRESIDENT IKEDA: Is that right? I met so many Soka Gakkai members on the train and on the platform. Some days I worked so hard that I wore myself out and had to take a taxi home. On those days, my wife or someone else would go to Kamata Station and pick up the bike I had parked there in the morning, so I could use it to get to the station again the next morning.

Drama in the Evening After Inauguration as President

MATSUOKA: The evening of the day you became president, a couple from Kansai, who were close acquaintances of yours, went to your house in Kobayashi-cho to congratulate you and celebrate. When they arrived, the house was quiet. As they opened the door to the entranceway, they saw it had been cleaned and sprinkled with fresh water in anticipation of guests. You came out and said: "I wonder if everyone is hesitating because now I'm president? Nobody has come to see me!" Then you invited them in.

SASAKI: When Mrs. Ikeda brought them tea and served it, you pointed to your wife and said with a smile: "We haven't had any celebrations here today. I was expecting a festive treat of rice with red beans, but she didn't prepare one! She didn't so much as say 'Congratulations.'" And you further related how you'd implored her, "At the very least, cook us some rice with red beans!" but that your wife had replied:

"I'm sorry, but I think of tonight as the funeral service for the Ikeda family. That's why I didn't prepare rice with red beans. There's no sea bream to celebrate, either."[38]

MATSUOKA: The couple from Kansai was surprised at how different from usual both of you seemed that night. They noticed that you in particular, Mrs. Ikeda, were not your usual smiling self but seemed very somber and reserved. In your unsmiling presence, they said they sensed a strong determination and resolution as if you were steeling yourself for what lay ahead.

MRS. IKEDA: I was resolved to face whatever happened from the moment I married my husband, but it is certainly true that when he became president our private life underwent a complete transformation. His public role and duties continued much as they had before, but now my private life, too, completely disappeared.

MATSUOKA: Mr. Sasaki and I once interviewed President Ikeda's mother, Ichi, some twenty years ago. We went to her home and, after we introduced ourselves as reporters for the *Seikyo Shimbun,* she kneeled on the tatami and, placing both her hands together in front of her in a gesture of formal greeting, said with great courtesy: "Thank you for supporting Daisaku. I hope you will continue to do so in the future."

SASAKI: We were so surprised, even embarrassed. We were so young and unimportant. But her action gave us a precious glimpse of the kind of family you grew up in. She emanated a most natural and refined dignity.

PRESIDENT IKEDA: From the time I began my apprenticeship with Mr. Toda, I hardly had a chance to see my mother. But she was always my mother, and she was always concerned about my health. She lived to be eighty, and just before she died, she said to me with a smile: "I have enjoyed my life. I have won."

Reside in a Palace of Life

MATSUOKA: Mrs. Ikeda, I wonder if you could tell us a little about the last years of your father, Shigeji Shiraki. He was so well loved by the members. They used to call him "Grandpa Shiraki." He joined the Soka Gakkai before the war, and he was greatly trusted by Mr. Toda for his steadfast faith. Mr. Toda wrote a poem for him:

> *As long as you are in Jonan [the southern part of Tokyo]*
> *I am confident*
> *Our citadel is safe*
> *On its solid foundation*

MRS. IKEDA: He lived to be eighty-five. About a year before he died, he caught a cold and from then on had to be confined to his bed occasionally. One day I had a call from my mother: "I'm worried. Your father is acting strange. He's saying things like, 'This coverlet is as soft as silk,' 'I'm in a beautiful forest,' and 'It's a palace.'"

PRESIDENT IKEDA: I was very busy at the time and couldn't visit him for awhile. When I finally managed to see him, he was resting underneath a cotton coverlet in a small room in his home. He conversed normally and seemed to be alert and in his right mind. Explaining his remarks to me with a satisfied smile, he said that sometimes he felt as if his surroundings were transformed. "This bedding is so comfortable, just as if it were a nobleman's silver-and-gold-silk-brocade quilt. And I can see a wonderful world—a field covered with flowers, and a beautiful forest glade filled with the sound of an indescribably beautiful melody. It's as wonderful as if I were in some sort of palace."

MATSUOKA: I can just see his kind, smiling face.

PRESIDENT IKEDA: I told my wife and mother-in-law not to worry: "He may be remembering something from a past existence, or be enjoying something that awaits him in the future. Perhaps he's experiencing the great joy he'll know in the future as a result of the great good fortune and benefit he has accumulated from the past and in this present existence. It's as if he's dwelling in the state of Buddhahood."

As Nichiren Daishonin says in his writings:

When you climb the mountain of perfect enlightenment and gaze around you in all directions, then to
your amazement you will see that the entire realm
of phenomena is the Land of Tranquil Light. The
ground will be of lapis lazuli, and the eight paths will
be set apart by golden ropes. Four kinds of flowers
will fall from the heavens, and music will resound
in the air. All Buddhas and bodhisattvas will be
present in complete joy, caressed by the breezes of
eternity, happiness, true self, and purity. The time is
fast approaching when we too will count ourselves
among their number. (WND-1, 761)

MRS. IKEDA: My mother, who thought my father was losing his wits, was tremendously relieved by my husband's
words of encouragement. Starting about ten years before
he died, each time he finished gongyo my father used to
open his copy of Nichiren's writings and read the passage,
"Although I and my disciples may encounter various difficulties, if we do not harbor doubts in our hearts, we will
as a matter of course attain Buddhahood" (WND-1, 283).
My mother joined the Soka Gakkai because her health was
poor, but as we noted earlier, she's still healthy and active
today.

SASAKI: Their stories give one a sense of the wondrous flow
of life from past to present and future, and the indestructible state of being that those who have persevered in their

Mr. and Mrs. Ikeda at Makiguchi Memorial Hall in Hachioji, Tokyo, September 2004.

faith all their lives attain without fail. Thank you for sharing them with us.

Lead a Life in the Way That You Can Proudly Say, "I Have Triumphed!"

MRS. IKEDA: I have been a member since I was an elementary school student. When I look back on my life now, I feel deeply, every day, just how wonderful Nichiren Buddhism is. It has the power to transform sadness into joy, and pain into gladness. It gives us the confidence to overcome whatever difficulties we may face.

PRESIDENT IKEDA: Mr. Toda frequently used to say that Buddhism enables us to savor life itself as the greatest joy. I think he was 100 percent right. Those who remain steadfast in their faith and work for kosen-rufu throughout their lives will, without fail, experience a happy and dignified death. I have come to this firm conclusion after years of experience with many, many people.

SASAKI: Power, wealth, fame, and learning are all powerless in the face of death.

PRESIDENT IKEDA: Yes. As Victor Hugo said, "We are all under sentence of death, but with a sort of indefinite reprieve."[39] We all want to face our final moments calm and composed and in triumph. That's what our faith is for. To die in sadness and sorrow, filled with regrets—that is death as defeat. I hope all our members will persevere in their faith and live in such a way that in the end they can say with pride and confidence, "I have triumphed." This is my wish and prayer for all my comrades.

Notes

1. Walt Whitman, *Leaves of Grass, 1860: The 150th Anniversary Facsimile Edition,* ed. Jason Stacy (Iowa City, Iowa: University of Iowa Press, 2009), 423.

2. As of 2015, Japan's life expectancy has reached eighty-four, according to the World Health Organization.

3. This dialogue began in late 1997, but as of 2014, 25.8 percent of the Japanese population is sixty-five or older, according to IndexMundi.com.

4. Leonardo da Vinci, *Leonardo da Vinci: Notebooks* (New York: Oxford University Press, 1952), 257.

5. The Lotus Sutra says, "As an expedient means I appear to enter nirvana" (LSOC, 271).

6. Yasushi Inoue (1907–91): A prolific Japanese journalist and author, who gained wide renown for his historical short stories and novels.

7. Daisaku Ikeda and Yasushi Inoue, *Letters of Four Seasons*, trans. Richard L. Gage (Tokyo and New York: Kodansha International, 1980), 93–94.

8. Serge Bramly, *Leonardo: The Artist and the Man,* trans. Sian Reynolds (London and New York: Penguin Books, 1991), 401.

9. Ibid.

10. Romain Rolland, *The Life of Tolstoy,* trans. Bernard Miall (London: T. Fischer Unwin, 1911), 234.

11. Available only in Japanese.

12. "Fufu de kizuku jinsei" (A Life Built by Husband and Wife), *Shufu no tomo* (Homemakers' Friend), January 1, 1990, 268.

13. Ibid.

14. *Makiguchi Tsunesaburo zenshu* (Collected Works of Tsunesaburo

Makiguchi) (Tokyo: Daisan Bummeisha, 1984), 8:406.

15. Ibid., 10:300.

16. The Open University of Japan: Formerly, the University of the Air. An educational institute providing degree courses only via TV, radio, or the Internet.

17. The Great Hanshin Earthquake, or Kobe Earthquake, occurred on January 17, 1995. It measured 7.3 on the Richter scale. More than sixty-four hundred people died and hundreds of thousands lost their homes.

18. *Beethoven: Letters, Journals and Conversations,* ed. and trans. Michael Hamburger (London: Thames and Hudson, 1951), 45.

19. Ms. Yamazaki died in 2006, fulfilling her dream of turning one hundred years old.

20. Jonathan Swift, *The Works of Jonathan Swift,* ed. Walter SCOTT (Edinburgh, Scotland: Archibald Constable and Co., 1814), 9:441.

21. Johann Wolfgang von Goethe, *West-Eastern Divan,* trans. J. Whaley (London: Oswald Wolff [Publishers] Ltd., 1819), 129.

22. Taminosuke Nuki, *Konworu Rii joshi no shogai to igyo* (The Life and Work of Mary Cornwall Legh) (Gumma, Japan: Konworu Rii Denki Kankokai, 1954).

23. Ibid., 108.

24. Ibid., 120–121.

25. Chang Shuhong and Daisaku Ikeda, *Tonko no kosai* (The Brilliance of Dunhuang) (Tokyo: Tokuma Shoten, 1990). Available only in Japanese and Chinese.

26. "The Book of Threes," *The Book of the Gradual Sayings (Anguttara-Nikaya); or More-Numbered Suttas,* trans. F. L. Woodward (London: Luzac & Company Ltd., 1970), 1:129–30.

27. Four meetings: A story appearing in many sutras about Shakyamuni's motives for renouncing the secular world. As the young Prince Siddhartha, he lived a very sheltered and pampered existence in the royal palace. Then one day, he is said to have ventured out of the four palace gates and encountered an elderly person, a sick person, a corpse, and a religious mendicant, respectively, on each excursion. These were his first disturbing meetings with the inescapable realities

of aging, sickness, and death, and finally, inspired by the serene dignity of the mendicant, he resolved to embark on a religious life and attain enlightenment.

28. SGI President Ikeda's speech is titled "Mahayana Buddhism and Twenty-first Century Civilization" and is found in *To My Dear Friends in America*, Third Ed. (Santa Monica, CA: World Tribune Press, 2012), 336.

29. *Nanden daizokyo*, J. Takakusa, ed. (Tokyo: Taisho Shinshu Daizokyo Publishing Society, 1935), 24:358.

30. Daisaku Ikeda, *Haha no uta* (Ode to Mothers) (Tokyo: Seikyo Shimbunsha, 1997). Available only in Japanese.

31. Daisaku Ikeda, *Humanism and the Art of Medicine* (Kuala Lumpur, Malaysia: SGI Malaysia, 1999).

32. Morton Puner, *To the Good Long Life: What We Know About Growing Old* (New York: Universe Books, 1974), 91.

33. Aleksandr A. Blok, "On the Field of Kulicovo," trans. Yevgeny Bonver, http://www.poetryloverspage.com/poets/blok/on_field_of_kulicovo.html.

34. The crane and tortoise are symbols of long life in East Asia.

35. Malibu Training Center: An SGI-USA facility operated from 1972 to 2003. SGI President Ikeda often stayed and held training and encouragement meetings there during his visits to the United States.

36. SGI President Ikeda himself received the title in 1996.

37. *Hiyoku* bird: A mythical bird with one body and two heads. Both of its mouths nourish the same body. See WND-1, 502.

38. Sea bream and rice with red beans are both traditionally served on festive occasions in Japan.

39. *From the Great Thoughts,* compiled by George Seldes (New York: Ballantine Books, 1985), 194.

Index

consistency from beginning to
end, 30
conviction, 14, 115
courage, 24, 69, 96, 126
Cousins, Norman, 4, 80

death, 16; Buddhist perspective
on, 6, 158
defeat, never give into, 137
Deng Yingchao, 61–62, 134
determination, 19, 28, 30, 47–48,
80, 82, 124, 138, 145, 153
dialogue, 7–9
"Dialogue With Nature"
(exhibition), 137
difficulties, overcoming, 104, 131,
156–57
Dogramaci, Ihsan, 72–73
Dunhuang, 62; Dunhuang Relics
Research Institute, 60

education, and happiness, 120
effort, 69, 98
elderly citizens, ix–x, 10, 68,
92, 96–100; compassion for
the, 67; environment for the,
74–75; strength of, 93
Elyutin, V.P., 135
encounter, seriousness of
every, 80
encouragement, importance of,
38, 85, 127, 129, 141
"Expedient Mean" chapter
(Lotus Sutra), 49

faith extending life, 71
Fang Minglun, 4
fostering, capable individuals,
122

four universal sufferings, trans-
forming, 46–47
Francis I, King of France, 5
friendship, 62–63, 110
Fukuoka Dome (Kyushu, Japan),
Asia Youth Peace Music Festival in, 92
fulfillment, 31, 108, 112

goal, 14, 45, 49, 51, 75, 108, 112
Goethe, Johann Wolfgang von, 49
gongyo (assiduous practice),
138–39
Gohonzon (object of devotion),
95, 119
good circumstances, creating, 2,
30, 94, 149–50, 155
gratitude, 17–18, 42, 98
Great Hanshin Earthquake, 34
Guam, inauguration and resolve
of SGI president in, 145
Guevara Romero, Juan de Dios,
50
Gulliver's Travels (Swift), 46
Gvishiani, Lyudmila, 83–84

Haha no uta (Ode to Mothers
essay), 68
happiness, 14, 26, 30, 44, 69, 96,
114, 155–56
happiness of others, 51
Harvard University, lecture at, 66
health, 93, 102, 117, 119–20, 125,
141, 154
Hong Kong Convention and
Exhibition Center, World
Peace Youth Culture Festival
in, 90
hope, 31, 80, 102, 126

Hugo, Victor, 158
human relationship, 100, 110
human revolution, 19, 66, 111
human rights, 25
Human Rights in the Twenty-first Century, 24
humanity, dedication to, 59

Ikeda, Hiromasa, 24, 139–40, 143
Ikeda, Kaneko, 62, 105, 113, 117; and Tsunesaburo Makiguchi, 114
Ikeda family, 113–15, 138–44, 154–56; shared commitment to kosen-rufu of, 116–19, 123–30, 133–37, 147–53
Ikeda, Shirohisa, 140, 143
Ikeda, Takahiro, 140, 142–43
Inoue, Yasushi, 6–7
Institute of High Energy Physics, 81
interactions, 74

Japan Professional Photographer's Society, 136
Jawaharlal Nehru University (New Delhi, India), 37
joy, 96, 127, 157–58
Juan Carlos I, King of Spain, 147–48

Kansai Soka Elementary School, 144
Kant, Immanuel, 26
Keio University, 143
Kinjo, Hideko, 92, 94–95
Kinjo, Hifumi, 91–92, 95
Kissinger, Henry, 4, 15–16
Kitazume, Masanori, 34

Kohagura, Toyo, 92
kosen-rufu, x–xi, 2, 27–29, 68, 76, 87, 94–95, 114, 117, 130–31, 140, 142, 144, 158; life dedicated to, 15, 63, 97–100, 112, 116, 122, 126; worldwide, 131
Kosygin, Aleksey N., 83

laughter, 73
leaders, 103–104, 115, 126, 128, 130, 148
learning, and political conflict, 82; dedicated to, 31–34, 36–37, 41, 60
legacy, leaving behind a, 121–22
Legh, Mary H. Cornwall, 53, 58–59; selflessness of, 54–57
Leonardo, da Vinci, 5–7, 10
Letter of Four Seasons (Inoue), 6
Li Chengxian, 60–62
life, Buddhist view of, 6, 29–30, 38, 49, 51, 64, 80, 86, 110, 112, 148–49; value creating, 93
life force, 99
listening, 127–28
Logunov, Anatoly, 81, 83
Loire Valley (France), 5
longevity, 100, 101–105, 107, 110; and family, 44–45; four-point motto for 75–76; secret to, 72
Lotus Sutra, 51, 99

Maeda, Yasu, 105
Malibu Training Center, 129
Makiguchi, Tsunesaburo, x, 25–26, 29, 33–34, 36, 51, 116, 119, 121, 144; leadership of, 115; and students, 120

Makiguchi Memorial Hall
(Tokyo), 63
Mandela, Nelson, 4, 24–25
March 16 Kosen-rufu Day, 27,
140
Matsushita, Konosuke, 21
Matsuura, Shinsaku, 41, 44
mementos, 84
mentor-disciple relationship, 28,
44, 116–17, 121–22, 125, 142
Miki, Jun, 136
Miki, Sumiko, 121
mission, 4, 27, 29, 63–64, 69, 95,
98, 117, 141
Mitsumori, Kunihiro, 110
Morita, Shuhei, 78
Moscow River, 135
Moscow State University, 81–82
Mount Everest, 63
myo (of Nam-myoho-renge-kyo),
30
Mystic Law (Nam-myoho-renge-
kyo), 63; sharing the, 128, 145

Nakada, Miki, 105
Nakama, Tamae, 96–100
Nam-myoho-renge-kyo, chant-
ing, 87, 125, 130; declaration
of, 139
Nanda, Ved Prakash, 112
Narayanan, K. R., 37
National Library of Foreign Lit-
erature (Moscow), 83; Soka
Gakkai corner at the, 85
National University of San Mar-
cos (Peru), 50
Niagara Falls, 54
Nichiren Daishonin, 11, 15,
30, 49, 89, 99, 106, 128, 139,

155–56; "On Establishing the
Correct Teaching for the Peace
of the Land" seven hundredth
anniversary, 89; on life, 109;
writings of, 35, 87
Nihon University Auditorium
(Ryogku, Tokyo), 150
Nuki, Taminosuke, 56

Ogasawara, Nagamasa, 45
Ogimi Village (Okinawa), 104;
neighborly values in, 106
Ojiri, Yoshihiko, 101, 104
Okinawa, 89, 99–100, 110; elderly
citizens of, 91, 93; Kachashi
dance of, 90–91; Okinawa
Chapter in, 97; Okinawa
Training Center in, 95–96,
105; Soka Gakkai in, 94, 111,
118; writing of *The Human
Revolution* novel in, 96
Open University of Japan, 32
opportunities, opening new, 130
optimism, 72, 80
Oshiro, Tooyo, 92, 94
Ota Ward, Tokyo, 114

Paris, SGI community center in,
18
peace, 145
Peace Preservation Law, 115
Peccei, Aurelio, 4, 18–19
perseverance, 69
pessimism, overcoming, 40, 103
Philippines, 147
photography, capturing nature's
beauty through, 135–36
physical activity, 104–105
pioneering, 124

plans, 3
positive forces, of the universe, 15
praise, importance of giving, 128, 131
prayer, 119, 130
present moment, importance of the, 28, 34, 137

Record of the Orally Transmitted Teaching, The, 15, 47
respect, 128
responsibility, sense of, 75
Rolland, Romaine, 13

Seikyo Shimbun, ix, 3, 22–23, 25, 35, 41, 70, 87, 92, 124, 133, 140, 153; "A New Century of Health: Buddhism and the Art of Medicine," 73
self-development, 81
Seligman, Martin, 102–103
self-improvement, 81
selflessness, 59, 98
Seneca, Lucius Annaeus (Roman philosopher), 92
senility, 101; preventing, 74–75
SGI, 21–22; members of the, 21, 56
SGI activities, 2–3
Shakyamuni, 47; "four meetings" event of, 65; overcoming "the three forms of pride" 65–66
Shanghai University, 3
Shima, Carlos K., 50
Shimmen, Masashi, 45
Shiraki, Shigeji (father of Kaneko Ikeda), 154–55

Shirokane Elementary School, 119–21
Sholokhov, Mikhail A., 4, 14–15
Silk Road, 62
smile, 124, 149
society, building a better, 21, 26, 46, 51, 56, 66, 69–70, 106–108, 110
Soka Gakkai (Value Creation Society), 21, 26, 28, 109–10, 114, 124, 126, 128, 140–41, 144, 151, 156; activities of the, 103; doctor's division of the, 74; inauguration of the third president of the, 150; Many Treasures Group of the, 2–3; members of the, 76, 96, 158; model for the, 115; nurses group of the, 74; pioneer members of the, x–xi, 3, 59, 68–70, 86–87, 94–95, 116; science and academic division of the, 101; as third president of the, 89
Soka Gakkai activities, 97, 111, 142
Soka Kyoiku Gakkai (Value-Creating Education Society), 25, 144. *See also* SGI
Soka University, 36, 143; correspondence education division of the, 31–33, 36–37, 39
Soka University Auditorium, Tolstoy statue at the, 13
Soviet Union [in 1974], 124
strength, 85, 115
stress, dealing with, 103–104
student division, 137
Sudo, Kiyo, 119–21